A-Z JAPANESE PERFORMANCE CARS

A-Z JAPANESE PERFORMANCE CARS

By Chris Rees

Herridge & Sons

Published in 2005 by
Herridge & Sons Ltd
Lower Forda, Shebbear,
Beaworthy, Devon EX21 5SY

© Copyright Chris Rees 2005

Designed by Ray Leaning

All rights reserved. No part of this publication may be reproduced in any form or by any means without the prior permission of the publisher.

ISBN 0-9541063-7-7
Printed in China

Picture Acknowledgments

I'd like to thank all the press offices which helped with the sourcing of illustrations for the book, in particular Arthur Fairley and David Finch at Subaru (UK), Lawrence Pearce at Honda UK, Denni Frater and Laura Cole at Mazda UK, Jodie Gooding at Mitsubishi UK, David Crouch at Toyota (GB) and Terry Steeden at Nissan UK. I'd also like to thank photographer Daniel Pullen, with whom I had the pleasure of working with at *Car Import Guide* magazine, several of whose excellent images appear in this book.

CONTENTS

INTRODUCTION	**6**
DAIHATSU	**10**
HONDA	**13**
ISUZU	**44**
MAZDA	**45**
MITSUBISHI	**78**
NISSAN	**109**
SUBARU	**136**
SUZUKI	**161**
TOYOTA	**162**
SPECIALISTS	**191**

INTRODUCTION
THE RISE AND RISE OF THE JAPANESE PERFORMANCE CAR

One of Japan's first-ever sports cars: the 1962 Datsun Fairlady was a convincing MGB rival.

If you said the words "Japanese" and "performance car" in the same sentence 25 years ago, bemusement would have been an entirely natural response. At the time, Japan was making technically backward-looking cars with scant enthusiast desirability. Yet today, some of the world's most potent and most highly regarded performance cars are Japanese.

How did this happen? Japan's rise as a car making nation has been remarkable. In the early days, Japan's inward-looking perspective meant that it concentrated entirely on its home market, with wholly derivative offerings.

Japan's great industrial giants were formed surprisingly early: Nissan's forerunner created its first car in 1914, Mitsubishi followed in 1917 and Toyota in 1935. After the war, Japan turned to western countries for aid and inspiration and most manufacturers produced versions of European cars through the 1950s.

The dawn of the 1960s saw Japan coming of age as a car producing nation in its own right. All Japanese companies began making domestic designs which, while recognisably Japanese, nevertheless drew all their inspiration from European and American designs.

Early attempts at Japanese sports cars were unconvincing, yet showed promise. Nissan launched its Fairlady open two-seater as early as 1959 but it was ugly, underpowered and poor around corners. With the 1962 Fairlady, Nissan had a car to match the MGB. But it was the 1969 Fairlady Z – known as the 240Z in export markets – that ignited the touch paper and can properly be regarded as the father of the Japanese performance car. The 240Z became the world's best-selling sports car, catapulted ahead by its lithe looks, keen handling and bargain price.

Toyota had proffered the delectable but high-brow 2000GT in 1965 but it was the Celica range, first seen in 1970, that led Toyota to its first commercial success with a sporty car. Toyota's greatest hit yet was, however, the MR2 of 1984: Japan's first-ever mid-engined car and a brilliant driver's car.

Mazda followed suit with the RX-7, a rotary-engined coupé that trumped even the 240Z in sales terms. Like many Japanese companies, Mitsubishi responded with more and more powerful coupés such

The first true mass appeal Japanese performance car was the Datsun 240Z, which became the world's best-selling sports car during the 1970s.

as the Starion, through the 1980s.

But there is one pivotal moment at which, it's no overstatement to say, Japan ruled the world. For a magical year or so at the turn of the decade into the 1990s, Japan's performance cars really came of age, turning from technologically brilliant but stylistically challenged, to objects of genuine desire.

Heading the charge was the 1989 Mazda MX-5, a car genuinely closer to perfection than almost any other. Mazda dissected what made British sports cars of the 1960s great, melded it with modern technical know-how and gave birth to the best roadster the world has ever seen – and that's not hyperbole, it's a fact.

Another example: compare the flaccid, lumpen 1980s Nissan 300ZX with the startlingly handsome and fine-handling successor that burst on the scene in 1989. Here was a car in which Japanese engineers learned Europe's handling secrets, then blended them with good looks, superior build quality and peerless reliability.

And then there was Toyota's new high-end brand, Lexus, launched in 1988 and especially the SC coupé series launched in 1991. And how about Honda's NSX, also launched in 1991, which heralded Japan's arrival – and a convincing one at that – in the supercar fold.

In short, by the end of the 1980s, Japan had grown up from being a nation that made highly technical cars with terrible chassis and numpty body styling to a self-confident force producing quality machinery that looked, felt and drove as well as Europe's best. Indeed it took several years for European manufacturers to respond.

When they did, Japanese cars were ready to take things on to the next level. Like the rest of the car manufacturing world, Japan discovered turbocharging in a major way in the 1980s. Turbocharging was a way to extract significant increases in power from small-capacity engines without huge expense. The trouble was, early turbo efforts were unsatisfactory to say the least. While they were fast, performance only came on strong after a long spool-up of the exhaust turbocharger (so-called turbo lag), while there were also early relia-

In the realm of exotica, Toyota produced the delectable 2000GT from 1965. This was a rarefied, high performance car sold in tiny numbers.

INTRODUCTION

Mazda's RX-7 of 1978 very much followed in the footsteps of the Datsun 240Z by becoming a best-seller. Uniquely, the RX series was powered by rotary engines.

bility problems and poor fuel consumption to contend with. However by the 1990s, many of these problems were beginning to be addressed. The turbo readily allowed engines to be tuned up to 280PS – the maximum power output allowed by a "gentleman's agreement" between car makers and the Japanese government.

While many of Japan's technological high-performance ideas of the 1980s proved to be relative dead ends – electronic four-wheel steering, active suspension and so on – one idea that did stick was permanent four-wheel drive in a performance context.

Combining a turbocharger and four-wheel drive was devastatingly effective, as Audi had already proved with its quattro. But it was left to Japanese companies in the 1990s to exploit the full potential of this trailblazer.

1989 was significant for yet another newcomer: Nissan's Skyline GT-R R32. This was the first time that a turbocharged engine had been combined with such effect in a four-wheel drive Japanese coupé. Enthusiasts came to call the GT-R "Godzilla" for obvious reasons – here was a phenomenally quick, capable, grippy car with unbelievable potential for tuning.

Yet the GT-R was more expensive than most enthusiasts could afford. It was left to Subaru to create an affordable 4x4 turbo icon – the 1992 Impreza. More than any other car of the 1990s, the Subaru Impreza brought performance motoring to the common man. It could out-accelerate contemporary Ferraris, out-corner most sports cars of the era and yet cost little more than a medium-sized family car.

At the same time as Subaru was conquering the world rally stages and world markets, Mitsubishi stepped up to the mark and went to head-to-head with Subaru with its Lancer Evolution. If ever there were a case of competition sharpening the breed, the decade-

A pivotal moment in the story of the Japanese performance car: the year is 1989 and Mazda launches the MX-5, probably the most perfectly executed sports car ever conceived.

INTRODUCTION

With its turbocharged engine, tenacious four-wheel drive and understated saloon styling, Subaru's Impreza – seen here in 1992 WRX spec – defined the accessible Japanese performance car for a whole generation.

It's often thought that Japanese manufacturers' involvement in international rallying is a relatively recent thing. This is a Datsun Bluebird on the 1965 Safari Rally.

long tussle between Subaru and Mitsubishi was it: as each one edged ahead in the driver appeal stakes, the other pulled another piece of magic out of the hat. Enthusiasts loved every minute.

Not all Japanese performance icons relied on turbocharging. With its Formula 1 footing, Honda was insistent on avoiding the turbocharger altogether. It put its faith in superior internal engineering and produced one of the all-time great systems in VTEC. Frequently exceeding 100PS per litre thanks to electronic variable valve timing and lift, VTEC reached amazing peaks of rev-happy delirium. Honda's S2000 sports car was red-lined at 9000rpm, while the world's best-ever hot hatchback was arguably the Civic Type R of 2001.

In *Japanese Performance Cars*, we have a huge spread of machinery, from tiny 660cc sports cars like the Honda Beat, through four-wheel drive icons like the Impreza, Evo and GT-R, right up to supercars like the NSX. On the way, we will discover Paris-Dakar rally escapees, Japanese performance icons with western badging (including Lotus, Porsche and AMG) and rare delicacies barely legal for road use.

I have not tried to make this book a definitive history of fast Japanese cars. Rather I have concentrated on the kinds of cars you are likely to come across for sale in local papers and enthusiast magazines. That means a rough cut-off point of the mid-1980s, co-incidentally the point at which Japan began making its most interesting machinery. In essence, the book is here to address a yawning gap in the motoring world: a reliable source of information about a broad cross-section of Japanese performance cars, many of which have never been written about in English before.

NOTE ABOUT POWER OUTPUTS

Throughout this book I have referred to power outputs using the European PS rating system. This is partly to maintain consistency in the book and partly because the PS system has become the standard for most markets. UK readers may be more familiar with the DIN bhp rating system, which is nearly identical (divide PS figures by 1.014 to achieve the DIN bhp figure). In Japan, the JIS rating system is used, which is broadly similar to the PS figure. Japanese outputs are widely used in this book with the "PS" suffix.

DAIHATSU

Daihatsu Charade GTti as launched in 1987.

Daihatsu Mira TR-XX Avanzato ZZ was sold in UK officially, briefly.

DAIHATSU

Daihatsu's speciality is city cars (or "K" cars). Effectively part of Toyota's empire, Daihatsu is not exactly well-known for its performance products, but that's not to say it doesn't have them. It has a history of racing and has produced a series of diminutive but exciting cars.

Can any Daihatsu really qualify as a Japanese performance car? Especially one with a 993cc three-cylinder engine? Well the **Charade GTti** (made 1987-93) was unique and charismatic, if nothing else. Its turbocharged triple engine pumped out 101PS at 6500rpm which, in its lightweight 810kg frame, delivered 0-60mph in an eyebrow-raising 8.0 seconds. It looked funky with its spoilers and semi-faired-in rear wheels and was a hoot to drive, if a little frenetic. In Japan there was also a Charade de Tomaso version.

Daihatsu has a tradition of making strange-looking microcars. One of the smartest was the **Opti**, first seen in 1992. This was perhaps best viewed as a modern Mini-Cooper, sporting a curvy, friendly shape with a sporty touch. Like most Japanese K cars, it was possible to buy one with a 64PS turbocharged engine and even four-wheel drive for extra grip.

The name **Cuore TR-XX Avanzato R4** may be longer than the car itself, but when you consider the hi-tech goodies overflowing from this pocket rocket,

Daihatsu Copen featured a folding hardtop.

The Charade de Tomaso version was only available in Japan.

you can excuse it the lengthy introduction. It had intercooled turbocharging, twin camshafts, 16 valves, permanent four-wheel drive, sports suspension, power steering, air conditioning and alloy wheels. A small number (around 50) were imported into the UK as an experiment but this was not repeated.

Daihatsu has enjoyed more international success with the **Copen**, a miniature convertible that fits Japan's city car dimension rulebook. It has a 64PS turbo engine, extraordinary looks and a clever folding electric hardtop. Some tuners in Japan have made them go pretty fast, though in standard guise they're not particularly quick.

The **YRV Turbo 130** had a 129PS engine, making it "the UK's most powerful 1.3-litre car." That meant 0-60mph in 8.1 seconds but this would have been better had Daihatsu not insisted on fitting automatic-only transmission.

Perhaps most startling of all Daihatsus is the incredible **Storia X4** (pronounced "cross-four"). It looks like an ordinary Daihatsu Sirion but inside there's a real rally car waiting to get out – it's got four-wheel drive and a tiny 713cc four-cylinder turbo engine designed to allow it to compete in domestic racing. Unbelievably it boasts 120PS at 7200rpm – that's no less than 168PS per litre – and the same engine has been tuned as high as 200PS! And it will rev to 9200rpm. The X4 also has an intercooler water spray, forged pistons, close-ratio gearbox and a stripped-out cabin.

Bizarre YRV Turbo 130 struggled with an auto gearbox.

HONDA
BEAT

1991-1996

Tiny Honda Beat had only 656cc.

SPECIFICATION

Engine	656cc 4-cyl
Max power	64PS @ 8100rpm
Torque	44lb ft (60Nm) @ 7000rpm
Transmission	5-speed manual
Brakes	Disc/disc
Length/Width/Height	3295/1395/1175mm
Weight	760kg

PERFORMANCE

Max speed (mph)	112mph
0-60mph (secs)	9.0
Fuel economy (mpg)	50
Desirability	★ ★
Availability	★ ★
Tuneability	★ ★

Can a 656cc microcar ever be called a performance machine? In the case of the remarkable Honda Beat, yes. This was Honda's second-ever mid-engined car (after the NSX) but this time it was all in miniature. Its tiny overhead cam triple-cylinder engine boasted 12 valves and a system called MTREC (Multi Throttle Responsive Engine Control system) that was derived from F1 technology. With 64PS at a hilarious-feeling 8100rpm, it boasted almost 100PS per litre with not a turbocharger in sight.

It may not have been the quickest car in a straight line but for handling agility there was little to beat it, thanks to MacPherson struts front and rear, balanced weight and light steering. All-wheel disc brakes kept things sharp too.

Standard equipment included air conditioning, electric windows and zebra-striped seats and/or mats. Steel wheels were standard but most cars will now have been fitted with alloys. Quite a few Beats have found their way to the UK as grey imports but watch for meticulous servicing – cambelts should be changed at least every 50,000km – torn soft-tops and rust spots.

HONDA CRX

1983-1992

Honda conjured up a cracking little hatchback coupe on the Civic floorpan to create the first CRX in 1983. Although the wheelbase was the same as the contemporary Civic hatchback, the chopped roofline meant that the rear seats were laughably small – this was effectively a two-seater.

Mechanically it borrowed its 1.5-litre 100PS engine from the Civic GT, which gave it GTI-style pace, while its front-drive handling was extremely sharp for its day.

In 1986 the engine grew to 1.6 litres and 125PS and the following year the CRX got a well-executed facelift which lengthened the nose and softened the lines, plus added an extra 5PS. In this form it continued until 1989 (in Europe 1990), when Honda launched its formidable 1.6 VTEC engine in the CRX. This featured electronic variable valve timing and lift and an ability to scream into the high revs, where all the power resided. And there was more of it – 148PS at an elevated 7600rpm.

Despite a total of over 700,000 CRXs being built, they are a rare sight today because rust was a perennial problem, insurance costs are high and servicing the VTEC engine can be expensive.

In 1989 Honda launched its 1.6 VTEC engine in the CRX.

HONDA CRX 1983-1992

Honda CRX: this is the second generation model from 1987.

The VTEC engine used electronic variable valve timing and lift to get 148PS at a screaming 7600rpm from only 1595cc.

SPECIFICATION	CRX	CRX 1600	CRX 1600 VTEC
Engine	1488cc 4-cyl	1590cc 4-cyl	1595cc 4-cyl
Max power	100PS @ 5750rpm	125PS (130PS from 1987) @ 6800rpm	148PS @ 7600rpm
Torque	96lb ft (130Nm) @ 4500rpm	105lb ft (143Nm) @ 5700rpm	107lb ft (145Nm) @ 7000rpm
Transmission	5-speed manual		
Brakes	Disc/drum	Disc/disc	Disc/disc
Length/Width/Height	3675/1626/1290mm	3675/1626/1290mm	3755/1675/1270mm
Weight	820kg	895kg	970kg
PERFORMANCE			
Max speed (mph)	115mph	125mph	140mph
0-60mph (secs)	8.5 secs	8.0 secs	7.2 secs
Fuel economy (mpg)	36mpg	35mpg	34mpg
Desirability	*	*	
Availability	*	*	
Tuneability	*	*	

HONDA
CRX/DEL SOL

1992-1999

Open-roofed 1993 Honda CRX (known as Del Sol in Japan).

This VTi had the option of the roof being retracted electronically.

With the Mk3 CRX of 1992 (called Del Sol in Japan and many other markets), Honda took a bold new direction that, ultimately, proved to be a blind alley. Gone was the 2+2 hatchback format, replaced by a prettier, strictly two-seater notchback.

It also boasted a removable targa roof. As a gimmicky option, you could even get the roof to retract electronically into the boot – the lid rose up on stilts and swallowed the roof as it moved backwards!

The UK got two versions: the ESi with a 125PS 1.6 engine and the VTi with a 160PS VTEC unit. The VTi also got ABS, rear disc brakes and stiffer suspension. The Japanese equivalent of the VTi was called SiR and had an extra 10PS plus the option of a four-speed automatic (never available in Britain). There was also an appealing 130PS 1.5-litre VTEC engine option in Japan. The VTi model was dropped in 1995 in the UK ahead of a small facelift in 1996. It left UK shores in 1998 but lasted a little longer elsewhere.

The CRX is great to drive, superbly built and very reliable. Watch for rust spots, clean engine oil, malfunctioning roof, worn tyres and interior wear.

SPECIFICATION	ESi	VTi
Engine	1595cc 4-cyl	1595cc 4-cyl
Max power	125PS @ 6500rpm	160PS @ 7600rpm (Japan 170PS)
Torque	104lb ft (142Nm) @ 5200rpm	110lb ft (150Nm) @ 7000rpm
Transmission	5-sp man or 4-sp auto	5-sp man (Japan also 4-sp auto)
Brakes	Vented disc/drum	Vented disc/solid disc
Length/Width/Height	4000/1695/1255mm	4000/1695/1255mm
Weight	1035kg	1090kg
PERFORMANCE		
Max speed (mph)	118mph	130mph
0-60mph (secs)	9.1 secs	7.7 secs
Fuel economy (mpg)	37	37
Desirability	* * *	
Availability	* * *	
Tuneability	* *	

HONDA CIVIC
VTi & SiR-II 1991-1996

1992 Civic looked genuinely sporty.

Honda had been edging towards the sporty end of the hatchback spectrum with its Civic but the fifth generation EG6 Civic of 1991 was certainly the sportiest yet. Indeed the three-door version sacrificed so much practicality for sporty looks that many pundits were openly critical. They had the wrong priorities.

Yes, the curious split tailgate was a daft idea and space inside was hardly generous. But where it counted – speed and handling – the Civic was near the top of the game. In VTi form (the only one worth looking at), the sizzling 1.6 VTEC engine boasted exactly 100PS per litre, unleashed at a heady 7600rpm. That was enough for 0-60mph in not much more than seven seconds. Independent suspension by double wishbones up front and a multilink rear ensured excellent handling.

The VTi was current in the UK between 1992 and 1996, in both three-door hatch and four-door saloon forms. In Japan the equivalent model was the SiR-II, which had an extra 10PS compared to the UK VTi and was also available with automatic transmission.

A full service history is essential to avoid expense later – frequent oil changes and cambelts every 60,000 miles. Check for intermittent tapping sounds, worn gearbox synchromesh, rusty rear arches, kerbed wheels and a full set of functioning warning lights.

SPECIFICATION		
	VTi	**SiR-II**
Engine	1595cc 4-cyl	1595cc 4-cyl
Max power	160PS @ 7600rpm	170PS @ 7800rpm
Torque	110lb ft (150Nm) @ 7000rpm	115lb ft (157Nm) @ 7300rpm
Transmission	5-sp man	5-sp man or 4-sp auto
Brakes	Vented disc/drum	Vented disc/solid disc
Length/Width/Height	4089/1695/1290mm	4089/1695/1290mm
Weight	1090kg	1090kg
PERFORMANCE		
Max speed (mph)	134mph	134mph
0-60mph (secs)	7.2 secs	7.1 secs
Fuel economy (mpg)	36mpg	36mpg
Desirability	*	*	*
Availability	*	*	*
Tuneability	*	*	*

HONDA CIVIC VTI 1996-2001

HONDA CIVIC

VTi 1996-2001

The 169PS 1.8-litre VTi was also available in Aerodeck estate form.

1.8 litres for 1997 Civic VTi, seen here in Jordan trim.

SPECIFICATION

	1.6 VTi 3-dr	1.8 VTi 5-dr
Engine	1595cc 4-cyl	1797cc 4-cyl
Max power	160PS @ 7600rpm	169PS @ 8200rpm
Torque	110lb ft (150Nm) @ 7000rpm	122lb ft (166Nm) @ 6300rpm
Transmission	5-speed manual	5-speed manual
Brakes	Disc/disc	Disc/disc
Length/Width/Height	4460/1695/1360	4460/1695/1360
Weight	1140kg	1190kg

PERFORMANCE

Max speed (mph)	128	138
0-60mph (secs)	8.0	8.1
Fuel economy (mpg)	32	30
Desirability	★	★
Availability	★ ★ ★	★ ★
Tuneability	★ ★	★ ★

The sixth generation Civic switched course again, back to a more sensible mainstream. Luckily Honda kept its B16A2 1.6-litre VTEC engine going in the new-shape car, still chucking out 160PS and redlining at 8000rpm. As ever, the VTEC's second wave of power did not arrive until 4500rpm. Handling was also exceptionally good for a front-wheel drive car, at the expense of some ride quality.

In the UK there was a Jordan special edition in Jordan F1 yellow paint but it was mechanically no different to the ordinary VTi. There was also a 1.8-litre VTi Civic from 1997 with an impressive 169PS but this was only offered in five-door hatchback or estate form, whereas the 1.6 VTi was fitted to the three-door hatch, four-door saloon and, from 1999, the two-door coupe.

Build quality remained superb with no rattles and uncanny reliability. Servicing must be rigidly adhered to, so always check the service history. Tuning is growing in popularity and turbos and superchargers are available to make an easy 200PS.

HONDA CIVIC
TYPE R 1997-2001

SPECIFICATION	
Engine	1595cc 4-cyl
Max power	185PS @ 8200rpm
Torque	118lb ft @ 7500rpm
Transmission	5-speed manual
Brakes	Disc/disc
Length/Width/Height	4185/1695/1360mm
Weight	1040-1070kg
PERFORMANCE	
Max speed (mph)	140
0-60mph (secs)	5.7
Fuel economy (mpg)	30
Desirability	★ ★ ★ ★
Availability	★ ★
Tuneability	★ ★ ★

1998 Honda Civic Type R sold only in Japan.

When Honda launched the new-generation Civic (EK-9) in 1996, most markets had to make do with the VTi, which was quick but not remotely in the same league as the Japanese Civic Type R. This slotted in as the third member of the "R" family after the NSX and Integra.

As with all Type R Hondas, the R stands for Racing. At its heart lay the latest VTEC engine, which boasted one of the highest specific outputs of any non-turbocharged engine on the road – its mere 1.6-litre capacity developed an astonishing 185PS, translating to 116PS per litre. That maximum output was delivered at no less than 8200rpm, while maximum torque (a poor 118lb ft) came up at a no less surprising 7500rpm.

Given these figures, it doesn't take a rocket scientist to realise that this was a car that you had to keep singing high up the rev band to get the best out of. The major benefit of doing so was a terrific soundtrack straight out of a racing car. With a power-to-weight ratio of 155PS per ton, this was one quick machine, easily beating its more senior Integra R stablemate in a straight shoot-out. Ultimately, though, it has to be said that the Integra was a more satisfying drive overall.

Spot a Type R by its deeper front spoiler, lower rear valance, wild tailgate spoiler and prominent Type R badging. It was also a lot lighter than standard Civics, had a stiffer bodyshell with extra bracing, tweaked suspension for a lower centre of gravity, torque-sensitive limited slip differential, bigger brake discs with sports tuned ABS and revised pedals for easier heel-and-toeing. Inside, the Type R had a Spartan but purposeful feel, including red Recaro seats, a Momo steering wheel, titanium gearknob and carbon fibre-effect instrument trim.

Sold only in Japan, there were two Type R models, both of them three-door hatchbacks. The first came with a full tally of luxuries, plus alloy wheels. The second followed the Japanese tradition for racing-style stripped-out models, having plain wheels, ordinary seats and a plastic steering wheel, managing to shave 40kg off the overall weight and gaining a little in the performance stakes. From December 1999, there was also a Civic Type Rx with body-coloured retractable electric door mirrors, keyless entry system and aluminium sports pedals.

All Type Rs will be grey imports so great care needs to be taken when buying. Look for a full service record, engine smoke and signs of any sort of racing career.

HONDA CIVIC
TYPE R 2001-date

New Civic Type R of 2001 was built in Britain.

SPECIFICATION		
	Europe	**Japan**
Engine	1998cc 4-cyl	1998cc 4-cyl
Max power	200PS @ 7400rpm	215PS @ 8000rpm
Torque	144lb ft (196Nm) @ 5900rpm	149lb ft (202Nm) @ 7000rpm
Transmission	6-speed manual	
Brakes	Vented disc/solid disc	
Length/Width/Height	4140/1695/1425mm	
Weight	1195kg	
PERFORMANCE		
Max speed (mph)	146	150
0-60mph (secs)	6.5	6.4
Fuel economy (mpg)	32	32
Desirability	* * * *	
Availability	* * * * *	
Tuneability	* * * *	

The so-called EP-3 Civic was the first to be sold officially in Type R form in Europe – indeed this Type R was historic in that it was exclusively built at Honda's Swindon factory. Even Japanese market cars were all built in Britain.

There is no doubt that the Civic Type R is an all-time classic. As usual, the Type R's heart was its i-VTEC engine technology, now combined with VTC (variable timing control) to improve combustion efficiency, reduce intake resistance and improve exhaust gas recirculation. The 2.0-litre powerplant offered 200PS at 7400rpm in EC guise (and 215PS in Japanese spec cars, which are invariably painted white).

The six-speed close-ratio gearbox (matched to a triple-cone clutch) was a delight to use, thanks to ultra-light action from the dash-mounted gear lever.

The Type R shell (three-door only) was stiffened up and the suspension got firmer dampers and springs,

HONDA CIVIC TYPE R 2001-DATE

Dash-mounted gear lever was ultra-fast.

Facelifted 2004 Type R got more power.

uprated anti-roll bars, 15mm lower ride height and 17-inch alloy wheels with 205/45 R17 tyres.

The car was extensively tested at the Nürburgring during development, and it showed. The chassis came alive on circuits, making the Type R an ideal track day choice, while on public roads it was scintillatingly quick. Only the steering feel and road noise were criticised in the press.

Aerodynamic aids included a new front spoiler, rear spoiler, side sills, rear suspension cover and new-shape door mirrors. A mesh front grille with "Type-R" script, black-plated headlamp reflectors and twin chrome tail pipes distinguished it, although most people agreed it was still no looker.

Inside, firm, bolstered seats, white dials, aluminium-effect gearknob and red Type-R logos helped it look the part. Air conditioning was optional and is very much favoured by used buyers.

From early 2004, the Type R got a mild facelift including new front bumper design, projector headlights, revised rear lamps and two-tone colour Recaro seats. Under the skin it got a lighter flywheel and clutch to reduce inertia and shave 0.2 secs off the 0-60mph time. Noise, vibration and harshness were also improved. The Type R was undoubtedly the pick of the Ford Focus-sized GTI brigade in the 'noughties.

The 215PS Japanese spec cars are always painted white. Here we see the first batch waiting to leave Honda's Swindon plant bound for Japan.

European spec Civic Type R's 2.0-litre VTEC engine gives 200PS at 7400rpm.

HONDA
INTEGRA
TYPE R 1995-2001

Rare four-door Integra Type R showing alternative headlamp design.

Honda's scintillating Type R badge really established itself with the Integra Type R. Buyers were astonished to find Formula 1 technology adding to the already-legendary VTEC engine system to produce one of the all-time great powerplants.

The third generation Integra series was launched in Japan in May 1993, based on the 1991-1996 Civic. It shared the same 2570mm wheelbase as the three-door Civic as well as its basic suspension layout, but it was a physically larger car.

The Integra's credentials as a sports coupe were apparent from the outset in the Si VTEC version, fitted with the same 1.8-litre engine found in the Civic VTi, developing 170PS at 7200rpm. There were also ESi (145PS) and ZXi (120PS) versions, but we'll hurry on past those.

The only version worthy of your attention is of course the Type R. The legendary Type R DC2 did not arrive in Japan until September 1995. Honda's stated objectives with the Type R were to achieve "brilliant acceleration, exceptional roadholding, fade-resistant disc brakes and unique style." The whole philosophy behind the development team was the pursuit of a racing car feel. By any standards, Honda succeeded spectacularly.

At the heart of it all was a quite phenomenal 1.8-litre engine. In Japanese spec it had 200PS on tap, giving it the highest specific output of any normally-aspirated roadgoing engine in the world at the time, at 111PS per litre. In addition to VTEC, it had Programmed Fuel Injection, high-compression, low-friction pistons, a big exhaust and hand-polished intake and exhaust ports. A close-ratio five-speed gearbox with a heavy-duty clutch and limited slip differential made sure the power was applied cleanly.

The Type R's legendary handling came about

HONDA INTEGRA TYPE R 1995-2001

'One of the greatest of all drivers' cars.'

through thousands of miles of circuit testing. The Civic-based all-round double wishbone suspension was lowered by 15mm and made much stiffer (it had a brace bar in the engine bay too). In combination with the limited slip diff, this was absolutely effective in minimising front-drive understeer – indeed many testers still reckon it is the best-handling front-wheel drive car ever made. Braking was by disc brakes all round with standard ABS, the front pair ventilated and shared with the NSX.

The Type R's slender weight of just 1080kg was achieved by cutting mass wherever possible. For example, a lighter flywheel was used, the driveshaft dampers were deleted, a thinner front windscreen was used, and there was a lightweight exhaust system and less sound insulation.

It all makes for one of the greatest drives ever. You can happily push the rev counter up to nearly 9000rpm, an exercise you'll want to repeat as often as possible thanks to an engine note that sounds like exactly like a banshee racing car above 6000rpm. The close-set gear ratios and low final drive deliver stunning acceleration, at the expense of cruising comfort. As for handling, the Integra feels super-stiff and extremely tenacious, offering a degree of balance and controllability that you won't match in any other front-

Honda Integra Type R sold in UK from 1998.

The Type R was initially only available in Championship White.

drive car. The brakes were best in class too. Downsides? It's a noisy beast, the fascia is a drab Civic leftover and there was some criticism of the steering.

Following the usual Japanese practice for competition-orientated machines, the Type R was initially only available in Championship White with white seven-spoke alloy wheels. The alloy wheel design was unique to the Type R, as were the dramatic rear spoiler, front spoiler and side skirts, all in body colour. In time, red and black paint were also made available (with black seats instead of the red ones in white-painted cars), and for the year 2000 yellow paint as well. Other than the seats, the cabin wasn't great-looking but it was reasonably practical, even if the fold-down rear seats were extremely small.

It took a while – until 1998 in fact – for Honda to realise that the appeal of the Integra Type R could extend to Europe. The European version had 190PS – slightly less than in Japan. Standard features of the European Type R included ABS, double airbags, leather steering wheel, carbon fibre-effect console and a titanium gearknob. Air conditioning was optional. In the UK the Type R was launched in January 1998 at £19,500, which was absolute bargain territory and it quickly established a cult following.

Meanwhile back in Japan, there were a couple of Type R variations. There had been a four-door Integra from launch, based on the 2620mm wheelbase platform of the four-door Civic. As well as a 170PS VTEC engine and even a four-wheel drive option, Honda

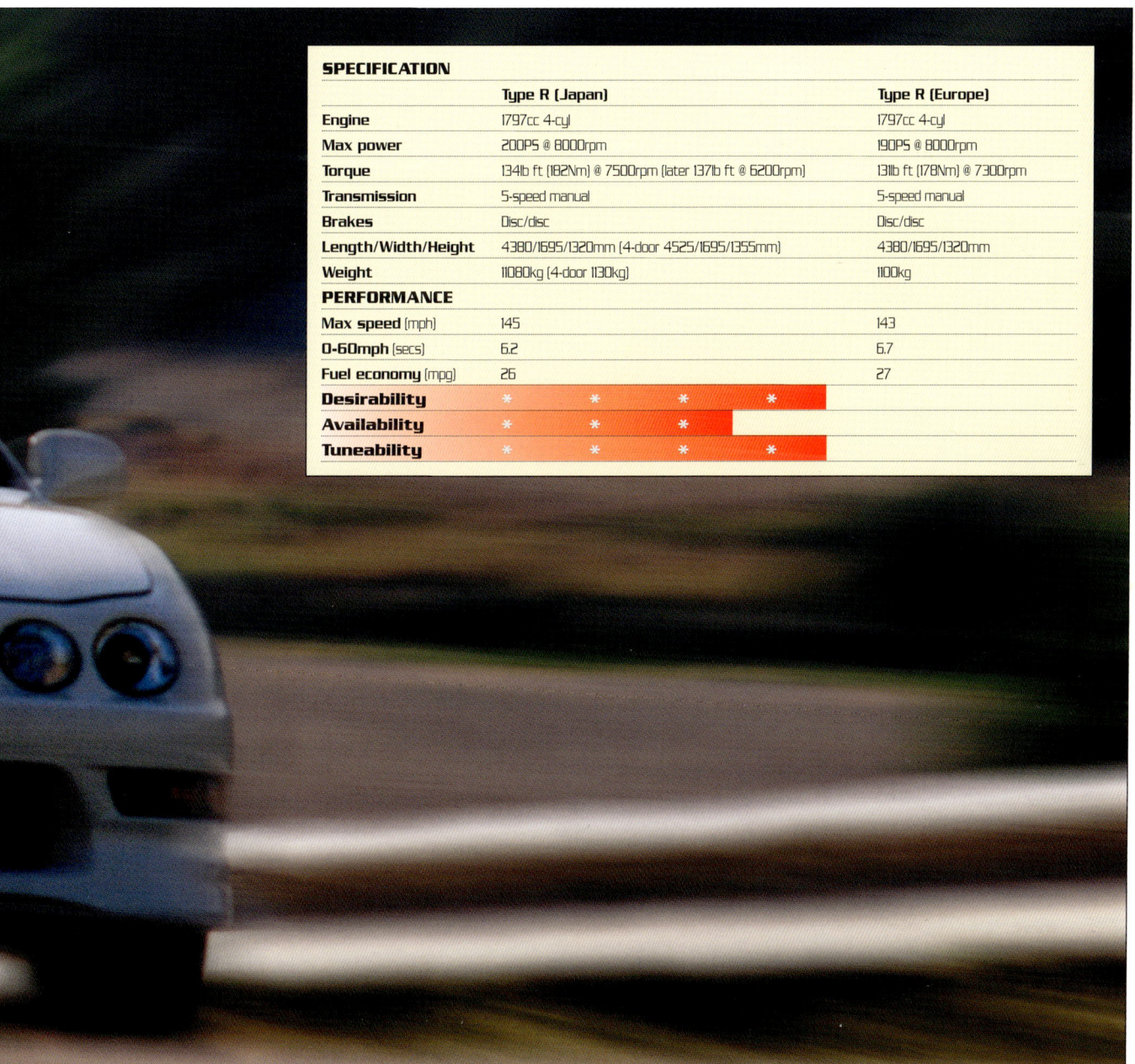

SPECIFICATION		
	Type R (Japan)	Type R (Europe)
Engine	1797cc 4-cyl	1797cc 4-cyl
Max power	200PS @ 8000rpm	190PS @ 8000rpm
Torque	134lb ft (182Nm) @ 7500rpm (later 137lb ft @ 6200rpm)	131lb ft (178Nm) @ 7300rpm
Transmission	5-speed manual	5-speed manual
Brakes	Disc/disc	Disc/disc
Length/Width/Height	4380/1695/1320mm (4-door 4525/1695/1355mm)	4380/1695/1320mm
Weight	1080kg (4-door 1130kg)	1100kg
PERFORMANCE		
Max speed (mph)	145	143
0-60mph (secs)	6.2	6.7
Fuel economy (mpg)	26	27
Desirability	* * * *	
Availability	* * *	
Tuneability	* * * *	

made a Type R version of the four-door, although its weight penalty of 50kg made it less of an enthusiast's choice. And in addition to the 200PS Type R, in Japan there was also a detuned 180PS version as well.

Changes were few during the Type R's production life. In January 1998, Japanese cars gained an equal-length four-into-one stainless steel exhaust manifold, which raised torque figures at low-to-mid rpm levels, while disc brake size and tyre size increased. Then in December 1999 (in Japan only), Honda added a special edition Type Rx to the range, which gained body-coloured retractable electric door mirrors, air conditioning, keyless entry, digital clock, electric aerial, aluminium drilled pedals, carbon-fibre style console trim, tinted rear glass and a special hi-fi. Some examples (Japan only) had a different, more conventional front end treatment with a new spoiler and rectangular headlamps. The Type R was withdrawn in 2001 ahead of an all-new Integra.

With such low suspension, look for damaged front spoiler and undertray and stone-chipped paint. Check carefully for signs of accident damage or heavy track day use. Tyre wear is heavy, especially at the front. As a specialist vehicle, a full and correct service history is vital – regular oil changes being particularly essential. Heavy brake use could mean scored, warped or worn discs. Tuning parts are quite readily available and the 1.8 engine can be taken fairly reliably to 230PS and even more with supercharging. The chassis can certainly handle it.

HONDA INTEGRA
TYPE R & ACURA RSX 2001-date

2.0-litre i-VTEC engine gave 220PS and was 10kg lighter than the old 1.8-litre unit.

The previous DC2 Integra Type R was a tough act to follow. Led by ex-Formula 1 engineers, Honda took a slightly different tack with its DC5 Integra Type R, launched in 2001, by giving it chunky new three-door styling, a larger engine and six speeds.

Its i-VTEC engine (dubbed K20A) grew to 2.0 litres to enable its power output to leap to 220PS. This was helped by variable intake/exhaust valve timing and variable timing control, plus high-strength connecting rods and crankshaft. The new engine was also 10kg lighter than the old B18C Type R unit.

A newly-developed close-ratio six-speed manual gearbox combined with an ultra-lightweight forged chrome-moly steel flywheel and helical limited slip diff.

The front suspension lower arms and rear brake calipers were in aluminium to reduce weight – the new model was only 80kg heavier than the old Integra – while torsional rigidity increased by 116%. The front brakes were jointly developed with Brembo.

The Integra Type R featured a deep front spoiler, side skirts, rear spoiler and spoked alloy wheels (17-inch in Japan, 16-inch in New Zealand). Inside there were Recaro front seats, Momo leather steering wheel and aluminium for the pedals, gearknob, handbrake lever and console trim.

The new Integra was not sold in Europe, while the Type R was only sold in Japan and, with 200PS, in New Zealand. A version did go on sale in the USA under the name Acura RSX. However this was not badged as the Type R but instead as the Type S, although it was close in spec to the Type R. It boasted 210PS but was rather heavier than the Japanese Type R.

In the USA a heavier, 210PS version of the Type R was marketed under the Acura brand as the RSX Type S.

Honda Integra Type R second generation launched in 2001.

SPECIFICATION	Type R (Japan)	Type R (NZ)	Acura RSX Type S (USA)
Engine	1998cc 4-cyl	1998cc 4-cyl	1998cc 4-cyl
Max power	220PS @ 8000rpm	200PS @ 7400rpm	210PS @ 7800rpm
Torque	152lb ft (206Nm) @ 7000rpm	141lb ft (192Nm) @ 6000rpm	143lb ft (194Nm) @ 7000rpm
Transmission	6-speed manual	6-speed manual	6-speed manual
Brakes	Disc/disc	Disc/disc	Disc/disc
Length/Width/Height	4380/1724/1394mm	4380/1724/1394mm	4380/1724/1394mm
Weight	1160kg	1190kg	1288kg
PERFORMANCE			
Max speed (mph)	150	150	150
0-60mph (secs)	6.8	7.2	7.2
Fuel economy (mpg)	29	29	29
Desirability	★★★		
Availability	★★		
Tuneability	★★★★		

HONDA
ACCORD
TYPE R 1998-2002

Rear wing and 17-inch alloys helped set the Type R apart from lesser Accords.

SPECIFICATION		
	Type R	Euro-R
Engine	2156cc 4-cyl	2156cc 4-cyl
Max power	212PS @ 7200rpm	220PS @ 7200rpm
Torque	158lb ft (215Nm) @ 6700rpm	163lb ft (221Nm) @ 6700rpm
Transmission	5-speed manual	5-speed manual
Brakes		
Length/Width/Height	4595/1750/1430mm	4680/1720/1405mm
Weight	1345kg	1330kg
PERFORMANCE		
Max speed (mph)	143	145
0-60mph (secs)	7.0	6.9
Fuel economy (mpg)	29	29
Desirability	* * *	
Availability	* *	
Tuneability	* * *	

Alongside higher-profile Type R Hondas like the Integra and Civic, the Accord Type R always struggled to make an impact. Based on the four-door saloon Accord, it didn't look much – a rear wing, 17-inch alloys and decals gave the game away – but that plain exterior hid a talented performance car.

The Accord's 2.2-litre four-cylinder VTEC engine – a development of the Prelude's – was typically high-revving: its red line sat at 7500rpm, with peak power of 212PS arriving at a screaming 7200rpm. The VTEC's second set of cam lobes provided extra boost past 5000rpm. Keeping the engine on the boil required concentration and frequent gearchanges from the close-ratio five-speed manual gearbox.

Chassis changes over the Accord included stiffer springs and dampers, lower ride height and a limited slip diff. Inside, there were Recaros, carbon-fibre effect trim and a titanium gearknob.

This was a very quick car around corners and one that Damon Hill rated highly (he had one as a company car). The steering was also highly praised, with torque steer absent. But the Type R was more expensive and slower than the Subaru Impreza Turbo and sales were slender. It's a great used buy though, and even boasts a low-ish insurance group.

Some mention ought to be made of the Japanese-market Accord Euro-R (GH-CL1), launched in July 2000 in Japan only. This was a misleading badge since the body was actually the American market Accord, not the European one. It got a 220PS version of the 2.2-litre engine with the expected uprated underpinnings: helical limited slip diff, stiff dampers and anti-roll bars, strut tower bar and 16-inch brakes. A Momo steering wheel and Recaro front seats were de rigueur. It lasted until 2002 when it was replaced by a new Euro-R.

First Honda Accord Type R was launched in 1998.

HONDA
ACCORD
EURO-R 2002-date

In October 2002, Honda launched its new generation Accord, a big advance on the old model. While in Europe the sportiest model was the 190bhp 2.4-litre Type S, in Japan there continued to be a Euro-R version. This was now powered not by the old 2.2-litre engine but by a version of Honda's 2.0-litre i-VTEC engine with 220PS at a screeching 8000rpm. Also new for this model was a lightweight six-speed gearbox.

The Euro-R was distinguishable externally by aero-form bumpers, honeycomb mesh grille, black-out headlights, titanium-coloured rear lights, dark-chrome plated door handles and 17-inch alloy wheels. As before, the springs, dampers, anti-roll bars and bushes were firmer. An uprated clutch, lightweight flywheel and limited slip diff made it a sharper drive. Inside, Recaro front seats, a Momo leather steering wheel, aluminium gear-knob and pedals and a metal-look console kept its sporty pretensions going.

If you want one, it will be strictly grey import only. You'll get a fast, practical car with well-sorted handling and you'll be guaranteed to be the only one on the block with one.

Japanese market Honda Accord Euro-R (2002).

SPECIFICATION	
Engine	1998cc 4-cyl
Max power	220PS @ 8000rpm
Torque	152lb ft (206Nm) @ 7000rpm
Transmission	6-speed manual
Brakes	Vented disc/solid disc
Length/Width/Height	4665/1760/1450mm
Weight	1390kg
PERFORMANCE	
Max speed (mph)	150
0-60mph (secs)	6.8
Fuel economy (mpg)	31
Desirability	* * *
Availability	* *
Tuneability	* * *

HONDA
PRELUDE

1991-1996

Honda launched the Prelude badge as far back 1978 as a coupé version of the Accord. Over the generations, it grew in size and introduced such novelties as rear-wheel steering. Honda launched its fourth generation Prelude in 1991 (UK 1992) – the first Prelude to look as good as it went.

Shorter, lower and wider than before, this was a stunning looking coupé for its time, featuring a very low front end and a curvaceously sporty roof-line. It sacrificed much to the great god of style as the rear seats and boot were particularly cramped. The cabin design was not much to write home about either.

Three engines were offered in European markets: a 2.0 (133PS), a 2.2 VTEC (185PS) and a new 2.3 (160PS). Even the non-VTEC units sounded urgent but the star of the range was undoubtedly the 2.2 VTEC (offered from 1993) with its searing high-rev power delivery and higher level of standard equipment (including air con and cruise control).

The more powerful engined versions featured electronic four-wheel steering that boosted grip and aided on-limit handling adjustability. The Prelude was a fine-handling machine, although the steering perhaps did not boast enough feel.

LCD back-lit instruments arrived in 1994 but the Prelude's shape had fallen out of fashion by 1996. Build quality and reliability were always excellent but parts prices look high and that VTEC engine needs careful maintenance.

The Prelude's 2.2-litre VTEC engine gave 185PS. The more powerful Prelude variants featured four-wheel steering.

SPECIFICATION

	2.0	2.2 VTEC	2.3
Engine	1997cc 4-cyl	2157cc 4-cyl	2259cc 4-cyl
Max power	133PS @ 5300rpm	185PS @ 6800rpm	160PS @ 5800rpm
Torque	132lb ft (179Nm) @ 5000rpm	156lb ft (212Nm) @ 5300rpm	156lb ft (212Nm) @ 5300rpm
Transmission	5-sp manual or 4-sp auto	5-sp manual	5-sp manual or 4-sp auto
Brakes	Vented disc/solid disc	Vented disc/solid disc	Vented disc/solid disc
Length/Width/Height	4440/1765/1290mm	4440/1765/1290mm	4440/1765/1290mm
Weight	1220kg	1305kg	1270kg

PERFORMANCE

	2.0	2.2 VTEC	2.3
Max speed (mph)	125	141	135
0-60mph (secs)	9.1	7.0	7.6
Fuel economy (mpg)	34	33	33
Desirability	*	* *	*
Availability	*	* *	* *
Tuneability	*	*	*

HONDA PRELUDE

1996-2000

Curvaceous styling gave way to edges in the 1996 Prelude.

SPECIFICATION	VTi (1996)	VTi (1999)
Engine	2157cc 4-cyl	2157cc 4-cyl
Max power	185PS @ 7000rpm	200PS @ 7100rpm
Torque	152lb ft (206Nm) @ 5300rpm	156lb ft (211Nm) @ 5250rpm
Transmission	5-speed manual or 4-speed auto	5-speed manual
Brakes	Disc/disc	Disc/disc
Length/Width/Height	4545/1750/1320mm	4545/1750/1320mm
Weight	1320kg	1320kg
PERFORMANCE		
Max speed (mph)	142	142
0-60mph (secs)	7.2	6.6
Fuel economy (mpg)	28	28
Desirability	* * *	
Availability	* * * *	
Tuneability	* * *	

After the swoopy fourth-generation Prelude, the 1996 fifth generation looked a little prissy, with its more conservative, rather boxy styling. It was a much bigger car, addressing criticisms of too little space in the previous Prelude, but it remained a sporty choice, at least if you went for the 185PS 2.2-litre VTi instead of the 133PS 2.0-litre.

As ever, the secret of the all-alloy engine's power was its VTEC system: beyond 5500rpm was where you saw most of the action. Four-wheel steering remained (an electronic system), while the double-wishbone suspension with gas damping was pretty sharp. Responses from the chassis were crisp and body roll was kept well under control, yet the ride quality remained excellent. As an alternative to five-speed manual transmission, you could opt for four-speed sequential sports shift automatic transmission, with F1-type button changes, but this was not one of the better such systems.

From 1999, the power output of the 2.2 VTi engine rose by 15PS to 200PS and a Motegi custom pack was launched for all models (body styling and new-design alloys). When the Prelude was retired in 2000, there was no direct successor and the badge disappeared from Honda's catalogue for good.

A four-speed sequential sports shift automatic gearbox, with F1-type button changes, was an optional alternative to the five-speed manual.

The 2.2 VTi engine originally produced 185PS but this rose to 200PS in 1999.

HONDA S2000

1999-date

SPECIFICATION

Engine	1997cc 4-cyl
Max power	240PS @ 8300rpm (Japan 250PS)
Torque	153lb ft (207Nm) @ 7500rpm (Japan 160lb ft)
Transmission	6-speed manual
Brakes	Disc/disc
Length/Width/Height	4135/1750/1285mm
Weight	1250kg

PERFORMANCE

Max speed (mph)	155
0-60mph (secs)	5.6
Fuel economy (mpg)	28
Desirability	★ ★ ★ ★
Availability	★ ★ ★
Tuneability	★ ★ ★

In 1999, Honda launched its first open-topped two-seater for three decades, and a storm of excitement greeted it. The new S2000 was so popular that the number of deposits taken led to a lottery system for potential owners taking delivery of their cars. Its specification was mouthwatering, including rear-wheel drive, sharp styling and a very special engine.

The new 1997cc four-cylinder engine slotted in as the most powerful member of the VTEC family, with fully 240PS. A red push button activated it and when extended it sounded raw, metallic and hard-edged. The red line was marked at no less than 9000rpm and the fireworks didn't really begin until 7000rpm. A six-speed gearbox kept the power on cam, boasting a wonderfully short-throw lever. All great fun but a bit tiring, perhaps.

The S2000 was clearly aimed at enthusiasts. While

Optional hardtop made the S2000 a practical all-year round car.

The classic sports car profile hides high-tech mechanicals.

VTEC technology taken to its highest level in this 240PS 2.0-litre engine.

the steering was fabulously fast-geared and the chassis was capable of extraordinary grip, some testers criticised it for ultimately lacking sharpness, while in wet conditions the tail was prone to suddenly snapping away – a real handful.

In July 2000, a Type V version with VGS (variable gear ratio steering) was launched for the Japanese market. This system electronically controlled the steering ratio according to speed, almost halving it to an incredible 1.4 turns at low speeds.

A GT version, offered from 2002, was merely an S2000 with a standard hardtop (a power soft-top was always standard). At the same time, the S2000's suspension was fine-tuned with increased spring rates, stiffer anti-roll bars and recalibrated dampers.

In late 2003, the S2000 got a facelift which included new front headlights, tail lamps, 17-inch alloy wheels, new bumpers and an interior makeover,

Business-like cockpit of the S2000.

as well as enhanced suspension and brakes.

In the final analysis there is no doubting the pure appeal of the S2000. It looks different to anything else on the road, has a wonderfully designed cabin, is well equipped and sounds like a racer when it's on song.

Reliability has been first-rate but insist on a full Honda history. Check for signs of accident damage, uneven tyre wear and be wary of anything less than a perfect gearchange.

HONDA NSX

1990-2005

If ever there was a Japanese company to make a supercar, Honda was it. And with its first supercar effort, the NSX, it came mighty close to the standards achieved by Porsche and Ferrari.

In so many ways, the NSX was extremely special. It was built at an all-new factory designed to allow craftsmen to hand-finish each example. It was developed with the help of Honda Formula 1 driver Ayrton Senna. And it was the world's first-ever all-aluminium production car.

Honda called for a lightweight, mid-engined two-seater. Not only the body/chassis monocoque was made from aluminium but the suspension and engine too. It ended up weighing 1370kg, remarkably light for a car of the NSX's performance potential.

Honda was especially proud of its new V6 engine. This 2977cc twin-cam V6 engine used VTEC variable valve timing to stunning effect, offering 280PS in most markets. It sounded sensational, revved like an F1 engine and offered super-sharp throttle response. The mid-mounted layout engendered peerless handling balance – there were really no handling gremlins. Indeed the NSX was superlatively easy to live with, as happy at 20mph as it was at 150mph.

While the NSX had just gone out of production after 14 years at the time of writing, looking virtually identical to when it started, it did evolve subtly. It was launched in Japan as early as 1990, in five-speed manual or, with less power, four-speed automatic forms. European markets got the NSX from 1991 with power steering arriving in 1993. In the USA meanwhile, the NSX was always badged as an Acura.

There was a Japan-only Type R model made from 1992-1995, featuring 120kg less weight because it had no air con, underseal, stereo or traction control and had lightweight seats. This early Type R also got stiff suspension, a lower final drive and a blueprinted engine. A slightly more refined development was the

Honda's NSX supercar was both extremely quick and practical.

The US-market NSX is badged as an Acura.

Type S (1997-2002) which was 45kg lighter than the standard NSX and had stiff suspension and Recaros.

In 1994 came the Type T targa-top NSX, which should be avoided as it compromises rigidity. New F-Matic "manual-feel" automatic transmission launched at the same time did little to improve the desirability of the automatic, which is frankly ponderous.

The biggest evolution came in 1997 when the manual transmission NSX got a larger 3.2-litre engine and a new six-speed gearbox. Responsiveness was improved and top speed increased from 162mph to 170mph. Brakes grew in size and there was a new front spoiler too.

At the end of 2001, the NSX finally got a makeover of sorts, but not much. The old pop-up headlamps were replaced by faired-in units, while air intakes and rear lights were revised and a taller carbon-fibre rear spoiler fitted. Inside, the Recaros were now partly in carbon-fibre. Under the skin, the front wheels grew to 17 inches while the rear tyres got wider and the suspension was altered slightly at the same time. This all helped deliver sharper handling and, said Honda, faster acceleration.

There was one final iteration of the NSX, a reborn Type R launched in 2002 (but only ever in Japan). Light weight was once again the key: carbon-fibre

HONDA NSX 1990-2005

NSX-R was the lightweight version (this is a 2004 model).

SPECIFICATION

	3.0	3.0 auto	3.2
Engine	2977cc V6	2977cc V6	3179cc V6
Max power	280PS @ 7300rpm	255PS @ 6800rpm	280PS @ 7300rpm
Torque	209lb ft (284Nm) @ 5400rpm	216lb ft (294Nm) @ 5400rpm	219lb ft (298Nm) @ 5300rpm
Transmission	-speed manual	4-speed auto	6-speed manual
Brakes	Disc/disc	Disc/disc	Disc/disc
Length/Width/Height	4425/1819/1170mm	4425/1819/1170mm	4425/1819/1170mm
Weight	1370kg (Type R 1250kg)	1410kg	1410kg (Type R 1320kg)

PERFORMANCE

	3.0	3.0 auto	3.2
Max speed (mph)	162	162	170
0-60mph (secs)	5.8	7.2	5.7
Fuel economy (mpg)	324	23	23
Desirability	* *	* * *	*
Availability	* *		
Tuneability	* *		

was widely used and Honda even fitted thinner glass and lightweight carpets to kill the kilos. Aerodynamics were helped by a new carbon-fibre bonnet, finned front under-cover, a rear diffuser and a carbon-fibre rear spoiler. Inside, you got Recaro carbon-fibre seats, a titanium gearknob and gear shift lights. The 3.2-litre engine was assembled to racing tolerances and balancing, and the drive-by-wire throttle was sharpened up. Handling was helped by hard-tuned suspension, a more rigid body, and lightweight forged aluminium BBS wheels with special tyres; braking efficiency was enhanced too.

The NSX continued in production until 2005 but at a tiny trickle. If you're looking to buy one, choice is limited and almost all are early examples. The good news is that Honda built the NSX to last. Provided you have a cast-iron service history, you should feel confident. Servicing costs are not at all frightening but some parts certainly are. Very few areas are weak but you should definitely check for clutch slip (clutches can last as little as 10,000 miles), suspension bushes, tyres, dented aluminium body panels and worn interiors.

NSX cabin was not quite in the Porsche league.

Subtle changes to the NSX bodywork in 2001 reduced the drag coefficient from 0.32 to 0.30.

ISUZU

1981 Piazza was derived from a Giugiaro design exercise.

Mention you drive an Isuzu and few people are likely to be very impressed. Isuzu is not a glamorous brand. Only the pretty Bertone-designed **117 Coupé** of 1968 held any interest in the early days but in the 1980s the **Piazza** arrived to liven things up. Isuzu can thank Giorgetto Giugiaro for that, for he designed the Ace of Clubs styling exercise on Isuzu mechanicals in the 1970s. Isuzu liked it so much that they put it into production virtually unaltered in 1981.

In character the Piazza was perhaps more style than substance, despite its all-independent suspension and 150PS intercooled turbo 2.0-litre engine. Its pace was decent (126mph and 0-60mph in 8.6 seconds) but its rear-drive chassis was outclassed, leading Isuzu to call in Lotus to sort out the handling ("Handling by Lotus" badges were then fitted). That improved things a lot, although never enough to make the Piazza desirable. Weaknesses include a rather tackily styled interior that tended to fall apart and a real dearth of parts nowadays. Imported to the UK from 1985 and dropped in 1990, Piazzas are extremely rare nowadays.

The only other Isuzu worthy of mention was the little-known **VehiCross**, an Isuzu concept car that actually entered production. Only 1000 of these wacky off-roaders were built each year for the US and Japanese markets and a handful have made it over to the UK as grey imports.

The VehiCross really was an extraordinary car, styled by a Brit, Simon Cox. Bolt-on lower panels made the painted steel bodywork above look streamlined, and with a steeply raked windscreen, it had sporting pretensions. Its 3.2-litre V6 engine had 215PS so, combined with a comparatively light weight, it was fairly quick (108mph and 0-60 in 9.2 seconds) and was actually quite fun to corner. The VehiCross may have had full four-wheel drive, but it was no off-road star. Inside was a mix of plastic and carbon-fibre effect trim, plus Recaro seats. Access to the back seats was limited because of the two-door layout but at least there were plenty of gadgets to keep you entertained, including a dash-mounted TV allied to a reversing camera. Novelty car? Absolutely.

Extraordinary Isuzu VehiCross merged sports car with SUV.

Bertone-designed 117 Coupé of 1968 was an early sporty Isuzu.

MAZDA 323

1600 Turbo 4x4 1985-1989

1985 Mazda 323 Turbo 4x4 (Familia in Japan) was one of the earliest turbo 4x4 hatches.

SPECIFICATION	
Engine	1597cc 4-cyl
Max power	150PS @ 6000rpm
Torque	144lb ft (195Nm) @ 5000rpm
Transmission	5-speed manual
Brakes	Disc/disc
Length/Width/Height	3990/1645/1390mm
Weight	1100kg
PERFORMANCE	
Max speed (mph)	124
0-60mph (secs)	8.1
Fuel economy (mpg)	31
Desirability	★ ★
Availability	★ ★
Tuneability	★ ★

Japan discovered permanent four-wheel drive and turbochargers in a big way in the 1980s and the Mazda 323 1600 Turbo 4x4 was one of the first. This three-door hatchback boasted permanent four-wheel drive and a 1.6-litre fuel-injected 16-valve engine, which developed 150PS in European tune, thanks to an IHI turbocharger. The 4x4 system was permanent and split 50/50 front/rear, with an optional rear limited slip diff in some markets.

It was launched in Japan in 1985, while in the UK it arrived in 1986 in two versions: the Turbo 4x4 Lux (with alloy wheels, sunroof and spoilers) and the Turbo 4x4 Rally (without the aforementioned extras). The Rally was available in limited numbers only and both versions were only sold until 1987. The Turbo 4x4 was then reintroduced for one year only in 1988 with black paintwork and stripes, plus items like electric windows, electric sunroof and radio/cassette.

Above left: In 1988 the UK Turbo 4x4 came with black paintwork with stripes.

Above: The Turbo 4x4 was a very effective rally car. This Group N car is taking part in the 1987 Welsh Rally. Works cars produced up to 250bhp.

MAZDA
323/Familia
Turbo & GT-R 1989-1994

The European spec GT-R had 189PS, whereas Japanese versions got 210PS.

February 1989 saw the launch of Mazda's seventh-generation 323 range (Familia in Japan), unusual in that it had two utterly distinct body styles: a conventional three-door hatch and a more adventurous five-door Fastback with pop-up headlamps.

It's worth mentioning the 323 1.8 GTI (later GT) front-wheel drive hatch with its non-turbo 140PS 1.8-litre engine. Unlike the previous three-door only Turbo 4x4, the GTI was sold in three-door hatch and five-door fastback forms, the latter with a double wing rear spoiler, and in some markets also as a four-door saloon.

Mazda's Turbo 4x4 model continued in this new generation in Japan and some European markets (though not Britain). In Japan (badged GT-X) it had a 180PS turbocharged 1.8-litre engine and four-wheel drive, in Europe a more humble 166PS. In 1991 the 323 range got a facelift, one year ahead of the launch in April 1992 of a powerful new 323 called the GT-R, designed to homologate the 323 for WRC rallying.

Based on the 4x4 GT-X, the GT-R got a more powerful "Big Turbo" engine, developing 189PS in Europe and 210PS in Japan. It looked a little more special too, with its bonnet louvres for the intercooler, prominent foglamps and a rear spoiler. It got full-time 4x4 with 43/57 front/rear torque distribution and viscous front and rear diffs, plus 15-inch alloys and a front strut brace. Only 2200 GT-Rs were made from 1992 until 1994, including 300 stripped-out competition examples with a larger front brace and rear strut brace.

SPECIFICATION

	Turbo/GT-X	GT-R
Engine	1839cc 4-cyl	1839cc 4-cyl
Max power	180PS @ 6000rpm (EU 166PS @ 5500rpm)	210PS @ 6000rpm (EU 189PS @ 6000rpm)
Torque	174lb ft (237Nm) @ 3000rpm (EU 161lb ft (219Nm))	184lb ft (250Nm) @ 4500rpm (EU 177lb ft (240Nm))
Transmission	5-speed manual	5-speed manual
Brakes	Vented disc/solid disc	Vented disc/solid disc
Length/Width/Height	4035/1675/1390mm	4080/1690/1390mm
Weight	1160kg	1210kg
PERFORMANCE		
Max speed (mph)	125	135
0-60mph (secs)	7.9	7.0
Fuel economy (mpg)	31	30
Desirability	★	★
Availability	★	
Tuneability	★	★ ★

MAZDA
MX-3

1991-1998

Mazda MX-3 had smallest V6 engine then in production.

Mazda's contribution to the world of small coupés was the MX-3 (sold as the Eunos Presso in Japan). Its main claim to fame was the fact that it came with the world's smallest V6 engine then in production (just 1.8 litres). Based on the platform of the humble Mazda 323, the front-wheel drive MX-3 was reasonably sharp to handle: crisp turn-in, little body roll and plenty of grip. The steering was quick-geared too at just 2.7 turns lock-to-lock. The usual choice was a five-speed manual, but initially there was also a four-speed manual for the four-cylinder engine, and in certain markets a four-speed automatic.

Mazda bucked convention with its ultra-compact 1845cc quad cam V6 engine, fitted exclusively to the MX-3. It sounded great with its twin cams, all-aluminium construction, four valves per cylinder and dual-ram induction with variable resonance injection. But its output was disappointing: 136PS could not even match Mazda's own 1.8-litre four-cylinder engine (which had 140PS). The V6 was instead about smoothness and an ability to rev right up to 7700rpm. Alternative engines were a 1.6-litre with 90PS (or 110PS with twin camshafts from 1994), and in Japan an interesting 1.5-litre twin cam engine in the early years, rated at up to 120PS.

Disappointments were the lack of performance, a nondescript dashboard and rather cramped interior, especially in the back.

SPECIFICATION	
Engine	1845cc V6
Max power	136PS @ 6800rpm
Torque	118lb ft (160NmNm) @ 5300rpm
Transmission	5-speed manual/4-speed auto
Brakes	Vented disc/solid disc
Length/Width/Height	4220/1695/1310mm
Weight	1110kg
PERFORMANCE	
Max speed (mph)	124
0-60mph (secs)	8.9
Fuel economy (mpg)	32
Desirability	* *
Availability	* *
Tuneability	* *

MAZDA
MX-5
1989-1997

The first-generation Mazda MX-5 launched in 1989 was a complete revelation.

Considering that sports cars as a breed died out in the early 1980s, Mazda was brave indeed to resurrect the genre single-handedly. And with the MX-5 (Miata in the USA), it scored the perfect distillation of the popular sports car – simple, affordable and fun to drive.

Almost half a million first-generation MX-5s were made between the car's launch at the Chicago Auto Show in 1989 and its replacement in 1997. Conceived at Mazda's Californian offshoot, the project was christened KISS ("Keep It Simple Stupid"). Mazda even drove and pulled apart a Triumph Spitfire and a Lotus Elan to see what made them tick.

The car Mazda came up with had unitary steel construction, with plastic nose and bumper sections and an aluminium bonnet. The design (by Tom Matano and Mark Jordan) was deliberately simple: uncluttered, classic and quite unlike anything then being produced. A charismatic feature was a pair of electrically-operated pop-up headlamps – just like the Elan. The soft-top, too, was a paragon of ease: swift to erect and stow.

The engine was initially the 1.6-litre twin cam 16V unit from the Mazda 323, with a lightened flywheel, electronic ignition, fuel injection and tuning to help it reach 7000rpm. Its power output was reasonable, if not potent, at 120PS. The five-speed transmission was ideal for the MX-5 with its close-set ratios.

As for the suspension, it got double wishbones front and rear, gas-filled dampers and anti-roll bars. Braking consisted of ventilated discs up front and solid discs at the rear. The steering was a rack-and-pinion system, although the optional speed-sensitive power assistance was entirely superfluous.

The MX-5 (or Miata in the USA) got a rapturous reception. *Road & Track* magazine in America called it

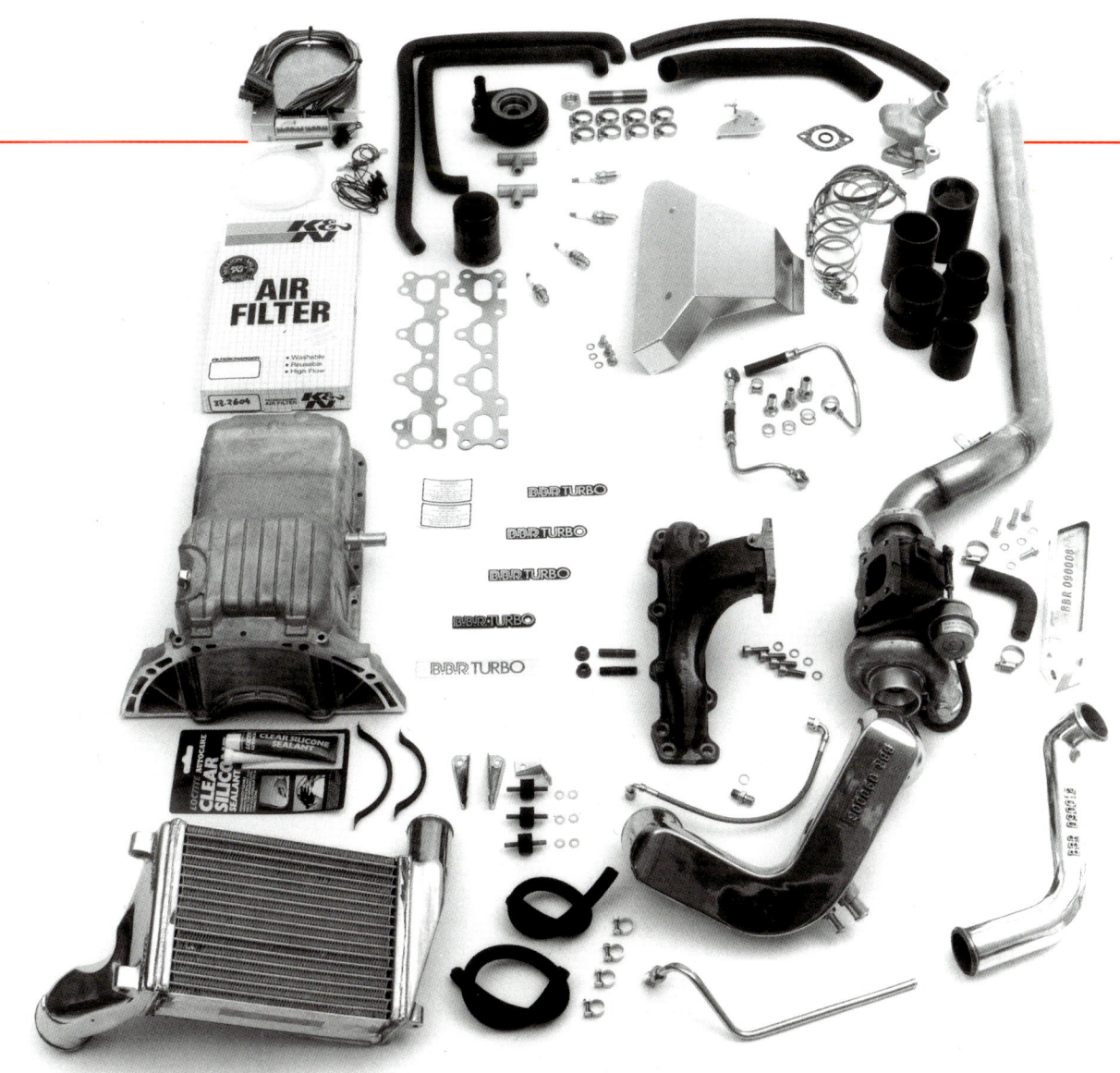

The factory approved BBR Turbo conversion boosted power of the 1.6 to 150bhp, or 230bhp with the BBR Stage 2 version.

SPECIFICATION	1.6 (1989-94)	1.8 (1993-97)	1.6 (1995-97)
Engine	1598cc 4-cyl	1839cc 4-cyl	1598cc 4-cyl
Max power	120PS @ 6500rpm (116PS catalyst)	130PS @ 6500rpm	90PS @ 6000rpm
Torque	101lb ft (137Nm) @ 5500rpm	112lb ft (152Nm) @ 5000rpm	95lb ft (129Nm) @ 4000rpm
Transmission	5-speed manual	5-speed manual	5-speed manual
Brakes	Disc/disc	Disc/disc	Disc/disc
Length/Width/Height	3950/1675/1225mm	3950/1675/1225mm	3950/1675/1225mm
Weight	955kg	990kg	965kg
PERFORMANCE			
Max speed (mph)	115	122	109
0-60mph (secs)	9	8.2	10.1
Fuel economy (mpg)	31	30	31
Desirability	*	*	*
Availability	*	*	* * *
Tuneability	*	*	* *

Uncomplicated interior followed the maxim "Keep It Simple Stupid".

"the best-handling two-seater in recent memory", praising the "quick and rigid response in steering, minimal camber change in cornering and wonderfully positive gear shift... It conjures up memories of the old Lotus Elan." In Britain *Autocar* magazine said: "Dynamically, everything from the gearbox to the steering is straight out of the top drawer... it is a more fitting successor to the Lotus Elan's crown than the new Elan will ever be. It is a total success." Criticism was restricted to the muted power output, noise levels and lack of equipment.

In Britain, concerns over a lack of power were addressed when Mazda UK approached Brodie Brittain Racing (BBR) to come up with an approved bolt-on turbocharger conversion, which boosted power to 150bhp (0-60 in 7.8 seconds, top speed 122mph). There was even a 230bhp BBR Stage 2 version.

Most mere mortals had to wait for Mazda's more powerful 1.8-litre MX-5 which arrived in 1994 in the UK. The larger 1839cc power unit was more powerful at 130PS but it had to cope with increased weight because of new safety equipment fitted, so performance was not drastically altered. A higher final drive raised the top speed to 122mph and the MX-5 got larger brakes, a limited slip diff and rear cross-brace. In Europe, the 1.6-litre engine was reintroduced as a cheaper entry-level model in 1995 but in detuned form with a disappointing 90PS on tap. In 1995, enhanced engine management and a lightened flywheel added 3-5PS to the 1.8-litre engine's output.

A large number of special editions were released in the UK but most were very forgettable. One exception was the Le Mans of 1991, which had a 150bhp turbo engine, spoilers and orange-and-green paint (only 24 made).

The first-generation MX-5 makes an excellent buy: well-made, reliable and long-lived. Prices are extremely reasonable and choice is huge. Check for a square rear numberplate which means the car is an imported Eunos (see next entry). Problems with pop-up headlamps can mean past accident damage. Check the fit and finish of soft and hard tops (if fitted). Unreliable central locking is a problem on post-1994 cars but don't necessarily worry about a notchy first-to-second gearchange on pre-1992 cars – it's quite normal.

Large number of MX-5 special editions were launched: this is a Gleneagles.

MAZDA EUNOS ROADSTER 1989-1997

It may be a bit of a mouthful, but the name Eunos Roadster has become a strong part of the motoring psyche. This was the Japanese market name for the first-generation MX-5. The Eunos badge was created for Mazda's sports and prestige models and Eunos cars were sold in Japan through special dealerships.

In almost all respects the Eunos was very similar to the Mazda MX-5 as sold in Europe. But there were some important differences. Some of the bodywork was different, notably the rear panel (with its square numberplate). The interior had some changes too – all of them good because Japanese market cars were so much better equipped. Much of the trim was different and you can often find equipment like wood detailing, speakers in the headrests and leather seats. Air conditioning was standard on all Roadsters and a hardtop was much more likely to be supplied with the car.

Mechanically the Roadster was very similar to the MX-5, but the engine management system was tailored differently, as was the brake balance. One very significant option available in Japan but never offered on European MX-5s was four-speed automatic transmission, but this really doesn't suit the car.

Mazda launched its new sports car in Japan in September 1989 (some months before the MX-5 hit UK shores), with a 120PS 1.6-litre engine. Side impact bars and driver's airbag became standard in 1992, the following year a 130PS 1.8-litre engine with larger brakes, limited slip diff and rear cross-brace, while a Series 2 model arrived in 1995 with light cosmetic changes.

There were a multitude of official variants and limited editions in Japan. These included the M2 1001 (130PS engine, roll cage and bodykit, 300 produced), the leather-and-wood trimmed V Special, the sporty RS and the run-out SR-Limited edition of 1997. Mazda's race/tuning wing Mazdaspeed also offered a bolt-on Eaton supercharger taking power up to 170PS in 1.6-litre form and 180PS with the 1.8-litre engine. Less spectacular tuning packages were also offered off-the-shelf.

The ultimate Mazdaspeed C-Spec model of 1997 is an MX-5 fan's delicacy. It featured a radically altered body with a single-piece front end and cowled headlamps, a retractable rear spoiler, widened tracks and much-revised suspension. Best of all was its expanded 2.0-litre engine delivering a remarkable 200PS at 7400rpm. The cost was vast (almost three times as much as a standard car) but it did represent the ultimate first-generation MX-5 model.

Don't be tempted by cars with after-market body kits and out-of-fashion alloy wheels – stick with as original a car as you can find. Most parts are readily obtainable, so your checks are pretty much the same as the MX-5. The best thing about an imported Roadster is its value – you get a far higher spec car for the same money as a UK-supplied car.

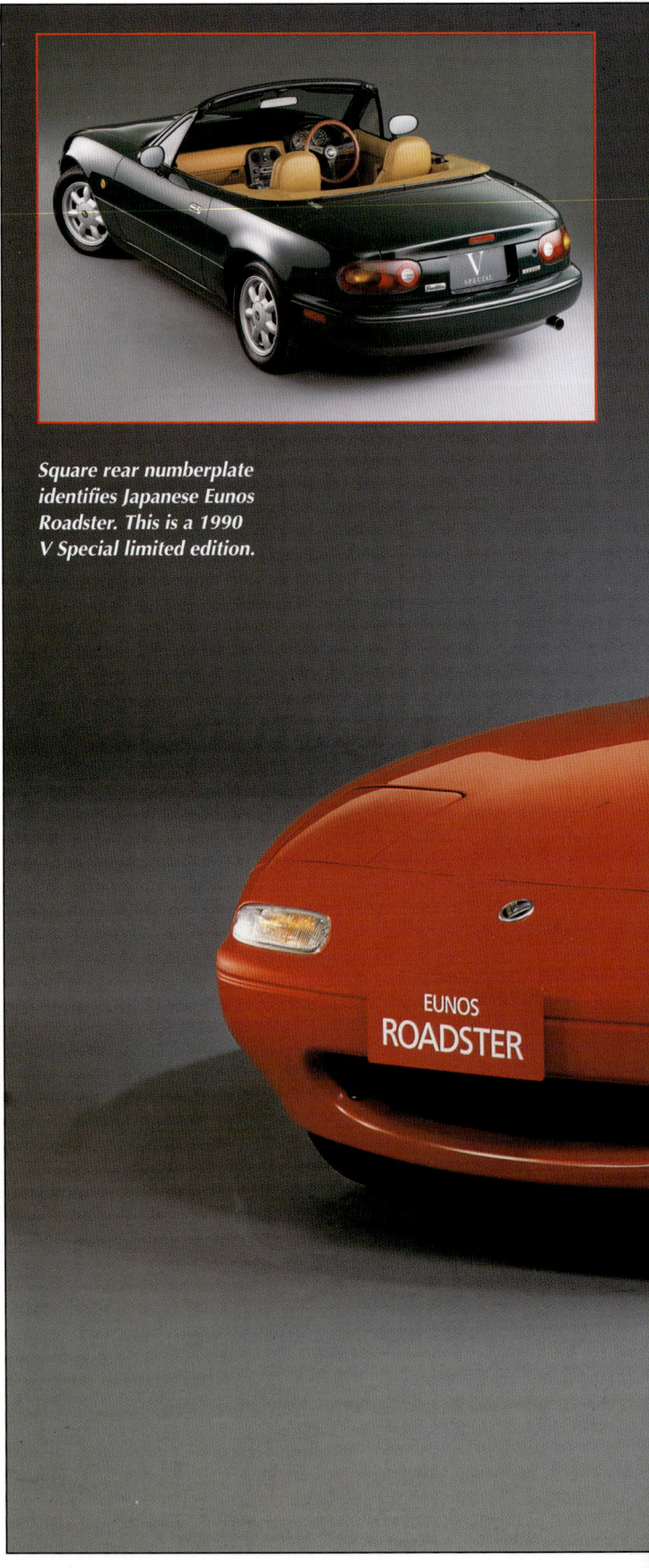

Square rear numberplate identifies Japanese Eunos Roadster. This is a 1990 V Special limited edition.

MAZDA EUNOS ROADSTER 1989-1997

In Japan the MX-5 was called Eunos Roadster.

MAZDA EUNOS ROADSTER 1989-1997

Eunos interiors were generally much plusher than export ones.

MAZDA EUNOS ROADSTER 1989-1997

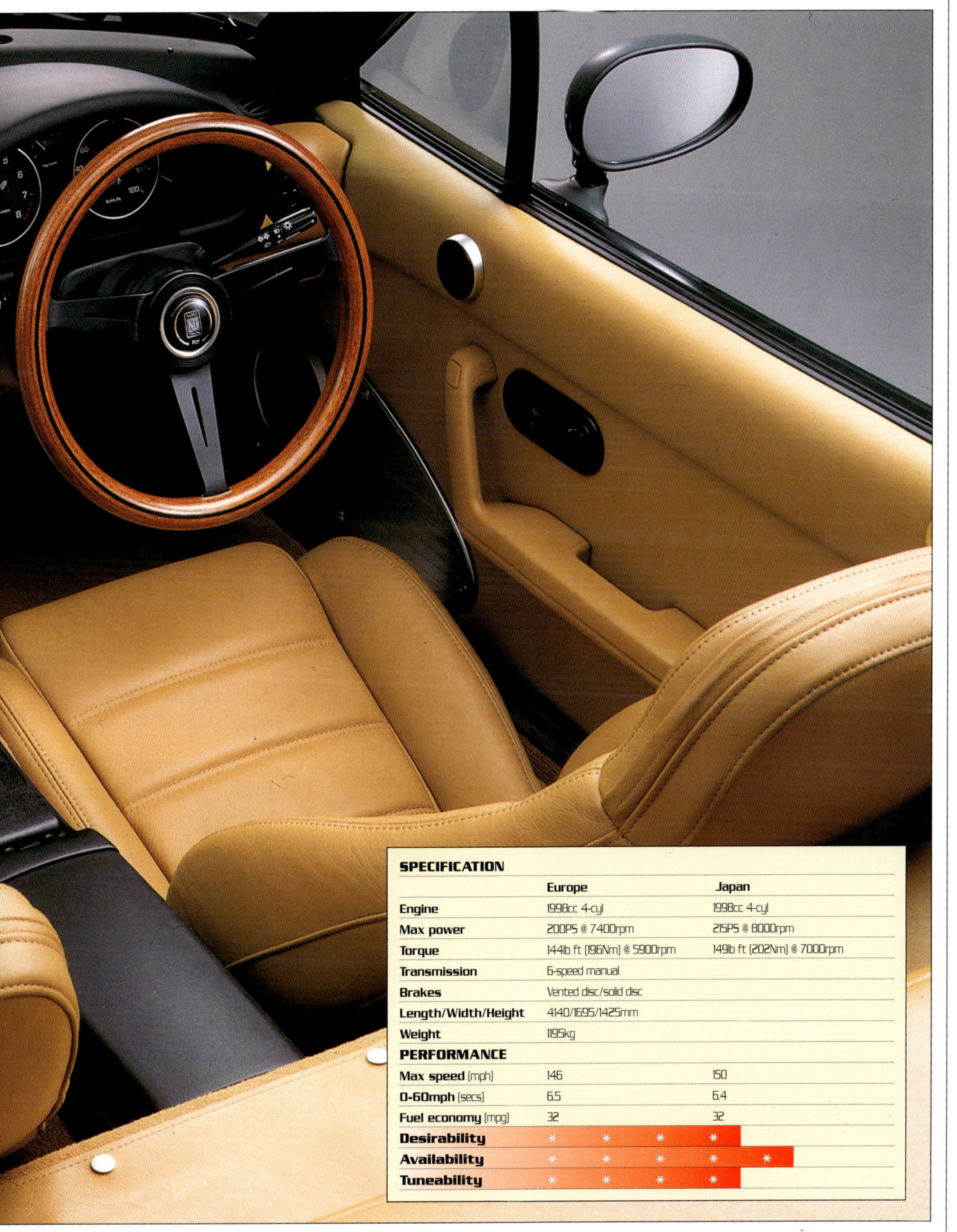

SPECIFICATION

	Europe	Japan
Engine	1998cc 4-cyl	1998cc 4-cyl
Max power	200PS @ 7400rpm	215PS @ 8000rpm
Torque	144lb ft (196Nm) @ 5900rpm	149lb ft (202Nm) @ 7000rpm
Transmission	6-speed manual	
Brakes	Vented disc/solid disc	
Length/Width/Height	4140/1695/1425mm	
Weight	1195kg	
PERFORMANCE		
Max speed (mph)	146	150
0-60mph (secs)	6.5	6.4
Fuel economy (mpg)	32	32
Desirability	★ ★ ★ ★	
Availability	★ ★ ★ ★ ★	
Tuneability	★ ★ ★ ★	

MAZDA MX-5

1997-2005

By the end of the first-generation MX-5's production cycle in 1997, Mazda was faced with an awesome task – to make what many viewed as a near-perfect car even better. And to most eyes, Mazda pulled it off. Most of the package remained exactly as before: the double wishbone suspension, the aluminium Power Plant Frame connecting the engine and final drive, even the wheelbase was identical. The soft-top (now with a standard glass rear window) and the hard-top were actually interchangeable with the original MX-5.

Externally the new MX-5 grew up. Although almost exactly the same size as before, the bodyshell was much stiffer, yet had not put on much extra weight. The styling was more muscular, taking a leaf out of the RX-7's book, with sculpted bulges along the flanks and on the bootlid. Most obviously, the MX-5 lost its trademark pop-up headlamps in favour of lighter, cheaper-to-make fixed units. Other detail changes included body-coloured door handles, bigger door mirrors and half-moon tail-lights.

The same-sized 1.8-litre engine remained under the bonnet but it gained an extra 10PS to take it to 140PS, with modifications including a new precision die-cast cylinder head, a better cam profile and a higher compression ratio. A new Variable Inertia Charge System changed the intake tract length above 5250rpm to improve induction. The 1.6-litre engine remained in the line-up as a budget option but it now developed a more realistic 110PS (though in certain European

Handling agility was what the MX-5 was all about.

Second-generation MX-5 launched in 1998 managed to improve on near-perfection.

markets a 90PS version remained available). Power steering was now standard on virtually all models.

In the UK there was initially only a five-speed manual transmission, but a six-speed gearbox finally arrived in the 1999 10th Anniversary Edition (which also boasted a body kit and superior equipment). Six speeds arrived in the standard line-up with the 1.8 Sport model of 2001.

The MX-5 has become the most popular roadster ever built, with its cumulative total (first and second generations) exceeding 700,000 in April 2004. It remains the archetypal sports car despite the arrival of numerous rivals, none of which is able to boast the sheer driving pleasure and the extraordinary value that the MX-5 offers. An all-new MX-5 was previewed at the March 2005 Geneva Motor Show and is described on page 60.

SPECIFICATION

	1.6	1.8
Engine	1598cc 4-cyl	1839cc 4-cyl
Max power	110PS @ 6500rpm	140PS @ 6500rpm (145PS from 2001)
Torque	99lb ft (134Nm) @ 5000rpm	119lb ft (161Nm) @ 4500rpm
Transmission	5-sp man	5 or 6-sp man
Brakes	Disc/disc	Disc/disc
Length/Width/Height	3975/1680/1225mm	3975/1680/1225mm
Weight	1015kg	1025kg

PERFORMANCE

Max speed (mph)	120	127
0-60mph (secs)	8.8	7.8
Fuel economy (mpg)	36	32
Desirability	★ ★ ★ ★	
Availability	★ ★ ★ ★ ★	
Tuneability	★ ★ ★ ★	

MAZDA ROADSTER

1997-2005

Japanese market second generation model was called simply Mazda Roadster.

In Japan the second-generation MX-5 remained badged as the Roadster (but now Mazda, not Eunos). The Japanese market offered many more model variations than were offered in Europe. For example, in 1999 there were five regular listed models. Like the previous generation, a grey import Roadster is likely to have leather upholstery, a Nardi wooden steering wheels and wood cockpit trim. Japanese market cars were always better equipped than the MX-5 in Britain, with standard air conditioning and alloy wheels.

The 1.8-litre model is the better choice over the 1.6, although both engines boasted higher outputs in Japan than in Europe. Opting

Pop-up headlamps gave way to fixed units. This car wears the optional hardtop.

MAZDA ROADSTER 1997-2005

In October 2003 Mazda launched the fixed-head Roadster Coupé. This car is in "Type E" spec.

for the 1.8 also opens up the possibility of choosing Mazda's wonderful close-ratio six-speed gearbox (on VS and RS models). Available from launch in Japan, the six-speed gearbox is something that arrived much later in UK MX-5s. Alternatively in Japan there was a new Aisin four-speed automatic, again unavailable officially in Europe. As the auto 'box is not familiar to dealers, servicing is more of an issue, while it's not the ideal choice for an MX-5 and could affect resale.

Japan and America also got the option of a Sports suspension set-up with Bilstein dampers, thicker anti-roll bars and firmer springs.

In October 2003, Mazda launched the Roadster Coupe, a fixed-roof version of the Roadster. This beefed up rigidity and hence handling. It was offered in four grades, of which the Type A was the most interesting, with its 160PS 1.8 engine and "racing" style bodykit. The Type E was an automatic with "classic" style front bumper.

Then in February 2004 came the limited-edition Roadster Turbo, the first official Turbo MX-5 in Japan. Power was up slightly to 172PS but torque was far better. Lowered suspension featured Bilstein dampers and 17-inch alloys and there was an aero bodykit. Only 350 were offered for sale.

SPECIFICATION

	1.6	1.8	1.8 Turbo
Engine	1598cc 4-cyl	1839cc 4-cyl	1839cc 4-cyl
Max power	125PS @ 6500rpm	145PS @ 6500rpm (later 160PS)	172PS @ 6000rpm
Torque	104lb ft (142Nm) @ 5000rpm	120lb ft (163Nm) @ 4500rpm (later 125lb ft (170Nm) @ 5000rpm)	154lb ft (209Nm) @ 5500rpm
Transmission	5-speed manual or 4-speed automatic	5 or 6-speed manual or 4-speed automatic	6-speed manual
Brakes	Disc/disc	Disc/disc	Disc/disc
Length/Width/Height	3975/1680/1225mm	3975/1680/1225mm	3975/1680/1225mm
Weight	1015kg	1025kg	1120kg
PERFORMANCE			
Max speed (mph)	122	127	137
0-60mph (secs)	8.8	7.8	6.8
Fuel economy (mpg)	31	30	29
Desirability	* * * *		
Availability	* * * * *		
Tuneability	* * * *		

MAZDA
MX-5

2005-date

The latest version of the MX-5 is bigger in every dimension and is 47 percent more torsionally rigid than its predecessor.

SPECIFICATION

	1.8	2.0
Engine	1798cc 4-cyl	1999cc 4-cyl
Max power	126PS @ 6500rpm	160PS @ 6700rpm
Torque	123lb ft (167Nm) at 4500rpm	138lb ft (188Nm) at 5000rpm
Transmission	5 or 6-speed manual (6-speed automatic in Japan)	
Brakes	Vented disc/solid disc	Vented disc/solid disc
Length/Width/Height	3995/1720/1245mm	3995/1720/1245mm
Weight	1075kg	1075kg

PERFORMANCE

Max speed (mph)	n/a	n/a
0-60mph (secs)	n/a	n/a
Fuel economy (mpg)	n/a	n/a
Desirability	* * * *	
Availability	* * * *	
Tuneability	* * * *	

After record-breaking sales, Mazda's MX-5 entered its third generation at the Geneva Motor Show in March 2005.

It remained a simple, lightweight, two-seater roadster but its fresh design and chassis drew on the acclaimed RX-8. It was bigger in all dimensions than the outgoing MX-5 (20mm longer, 40mm wider, 20mm taller and 65mm extra wheelbase length), but it was just 10kg heavier.

The old "Coke bottle" shape gave way to a straight-through waist-line. The headlamps were squarer, while a new oval air intake looked more striking in the shark-like nose.

The cockpit grew much wider, with better hip, shoulder and elbow room and space for side air bags. The dashboard had an RX-8 inspired centre console plus five individual circular gauges.

Under the bonnet, a choice of all-alloy 'MZR'

Mazda usually waits a few years before releasing a special edition. With the third-generation MX-5 the company launched the Limited Edition at the same time as the standard car. Only 3500 were built.

engines were derived from the Mazda6. The entry-level was a 1.8-litre unit (126PS), but far more exciting was a new 2.0-litre option with 160PS. These switched from cast-iron block to aluminium block and head. A lighter flywheel, electric throttle and a stiffer driveshaft made acceleration more responsive.

Significantly, the engine sat 135mm further back in the chassis, improving the front/rear weight balance. Aluminium was used extensively in the chassis to minimise unsprung weight, while overall the body was 47 percent more torsionally rigid.

Double wishbones up front were complemented by a multi-link rear end (the previous MX-5 had wishbones all round). Wider 205-section tyres offered more grip than the old MX-5, helped by wider front and rear tracks.

An all-new six-speed manual gearbox topped the range, with a five-speed manual for entry-level versions (plus a new six-speed paddle-shift automatic for Japan). Traction control was available for the first time in an MX-5, and brakes were bigger all round.

Production began in May 2005 ahead of an on-sale date of November 2005, with Mazda fully expecting its new generation MX-5 to sell even better than the old models.

The stylish interior features an RX-8 inspired centre console. An all new 6-speed gearbox is available.

MAZDA
MX-6

1992-1998

Mazda MX-6 was a big four-seater coupe based on the 626.

SPECIFICATION

Engine	2497cc V6
Max power	165PS @ 5600rpm (Japan 200PS @ 6500rpm)
Torque	160lb ft (217Nm) @ 4800rpm (Japan 165lb ft (224Nm) @ 5500rpm)
Transmission	5-speed manual or 4-speed automatic
Brakes	Vented disc/solid disc
Length/Width/Height	4615/1750/1310mm
Weight	1170kg

PERFORMANCE

Max speed (mph)	136
0-60mph (secs)	8.2
Fuel economy (mpg)	31
Desirability	✶ ✶
Availability	✶ ✶
Tuneability	✶ ✶

Picture the Mazda 626 and you automatically think of an anonymous medium-sized hatchback – if you can picture it at all. While Mazda always made coupé versions of the 626, it was not until the MX-6 of 1992 that it could claim it had a truly sporty four-seater coupé – even though the MX-6 was still based on the 626 platform.

That meant it had a lanky wheelbase and slightly ungainly appearance that looked like it should be a hatchback (it wasn't). The 626 basis also compromised handling somewhat: it was typical front-drive in many ways and, although it subdued torque steer very well, it lacked a truly sharp handling feel.

In the UK, only the 2.5-litre V6 engine was offered but European markets had a choice of 1.8 and 2.0-litre four-cylinder units as well, while Japan also had 1.8 and 2.0 V6 engine options. The MX-6 makes an unusual, practical and reliable choice but ultimately it lacks any real "wow" factor.

MAZDA RX-7

1978-1985

Mazda's RX-7 (Savanna in Japan) was an individual choice for 1978.

They say it's lonely at the top. Mazda should know, for it has been utterly isolated in its pursuit of the Wankel rotary engine for 25 years. Its persistence paid off with the RX-7 – a car which, it is no understatement to say, was one of the world's greatest and most significant sports cars.

Mazda dabbled with a whole range of rotary-powered cars in the 1970s but never really got into its stride until it tried putting a Wankel in a sports car. For 1978, the original RX-7 was simply a brilliant package – a true sports car with an extraordinary engine.

Launched in March 1978 as the Savanna RX-7 in Japan and just RX-7 in the rest of the world, this was to become the world's best-selling sports car in its day – a remarkable record because Mazda's previous rotary-engined efforts had bombed in world markets.

The RX-7 was designed from the outset to have universal appeal. The parameters were individual styling, 50/50 weight distribution (in fact it ended up as 54/46), a low centre of gravity, a comfortable interior, generous luggage space and as much componentry as possible taken from the RX-3 to keep costs down.

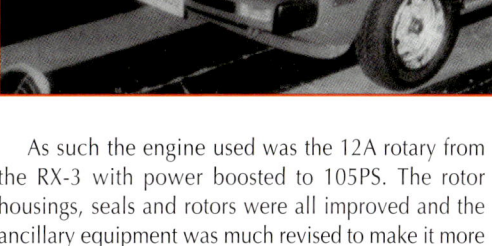

As such the engine used was the 12A rotary from the RX-3 with power boosted to 105PS. The rotor housings, seals and rotors were all improved and the ancillary equipment was much revised to make it more efficient, economical and durable.

Charismatic, high-revving and smooth, there was nothing like the RX-7. It was not particularly fast though. Mazda's claim of 0-60mph in 8.6 seconds and

The RX-7 was the world's best selling sports car in its day.

MAZDA RX-7 1978-1985

SPECIFICATION

	RX-7	RX-7 Turbo
Engine	2 x 573cc (equivalent to 2292cc)	2 x 573cc (equivalent to 2292cc)
Max power	105PS @ 6000rpm (later 115PS)	165PS @ 6500rpm
Torque	106lb ft (144Nm) @ 4000rpm	166lb ft (225Nm) @ 4000rpm
Transmission	5-speed manual (4-speed automatic available in Japan)	
Brakes	Vented disc/solid disc	Vented disc/solid disc
Length/Width/Height	4285/1675/1260mm	4285/1675/1260mm
Weight	1065kg	1100kg

PERFORMANCE

Max speed (mph)	115 (later 120)	143
0-60mph (secs)	10.1 (later 8.9)	7.5
Fuel economy (mpg)	26	20
Desirability	✷ ✷ ✷	
Availability	✷ ✷	
Tuneability	✷ ✷ ✷	

120mph were not confirmed by testers, who achieved more like 10 seconds and 115mph. It was entertaining though – possibly too entertaining if you were following one in the dark, since the engine had a tendency to back-fire when decelerating, despite the presence of an "anti-afterburn valve".

Under the skin it sounded disappointing: drum rear brakes, recirculating ball steering and a live rear axle. But in practice it worked extremely well, with mild understeer progressing to oversteer. The most serious complaint was the steering, which was far too slow-geared for a sports car.

This was an unusually clean-looking car for Japan in the 1970s. Pop-up headlamps kept the profile smooth and aerodynamic (Cd 0.34). The rear end was unusual too, with an all-glass upper section, the middle of which hinged upwards for access to a generously-sized boot.

RX-7 interior was a classic of design simplicity.

Smooth rear end with glass hatch helped keep the Cd down to 0.34.

In certain markets such as America, the RX-7 was a strict two-seater. But in others (including the UK) it had a tiny (in fact unusable) folding rear seat. Equipment levels were fairly stark but then it was bargain-priced in most markets.

A new nose arrived in 1980-81 and at the same time, many markets gained all-disc brakes and a narrower anti-roll bar to reduce oversteer, while power rose in the UK to 115PS. In 1983 ('84 in the UK) came the P132 series, with extra equipment, 14-inch alloy wheels, reshaped rotor seals, enlarged porting, repositioned plugs, ventilated rear discs and altered gearing. In the USA it got the bigger 13B engine and in Japan, a 165bhp turbocharged model was offered from this time. British drivers could turn to TWR, which offered a home-grown turbo installation.

An RX-7 is often seen as a risky buy because of its rotary engine, but modern technology and sound maintenance make the Wankel pretty reliable. High mileage engines may well need expensive work so pay less when buying. Your biggest problem is a dearth of good cars from which to choose – early cars are now pretty rare.

MAZDA RX-7

GENERATION II 1985-1991

Mazda's RX-7 MkII of 1986 grew up in size – and price.

While the original RX-7 sold well over 500,000 examples, the Generation II did less well, probably because it moved significantly upmarket. The Generation II was now aimed squarely at the Porsche 944.

The second-generation RX-7 (launched in Japan in September 1985) was larger, heavier and softer, therefore far less of a sports car and more of a boulevard cruiser. To cut weight, Mazda did use many alloy components, such as suspension arms, engine mounts, brake calipers and bonnet. Its bulky 1190kg weight was now however perfectly balanced over each axle.

The spec sheet looked more up-to-date with fully-independent suspension, four-wheel disc brakes and rack-and-pinion steering. The suspension even incorporated automatically adjustable dampers and a clever Dynamic Tracking Suspension System of floating hubs and multi-link pivoting – an early precursor to passive four-wheel steering.

It looked clean and was more aerodynamic (Cd 0.31); when the Sports Package was added (front air dam, skirts and rear spoiler), the Cd figure fell to 0.29 (this pack was optional on the non-turbo RX-7 and standard on the Turbo II).

Even with a larger 150PS 13B engine fitted, performance was held back by the weight. So Mazda developed a storming 185PS Turbo II version for Japan and the USA, fitted with a Hitachi twin-scroll turbocharger and intercooler and capable of 140mph.

SPECIFICATION

	RX-7	RX-7 Turbo
Engine	2 x 654cc (equivalent to 2616cc)	2 x 654cc (equivalent to 2616cc)
Max power	150PS @ 6500rpm	185PS @ 6500rpm (later 200PS)
Torque	134lb ft (182Nm) @ 3000rpm	180lb ft (244Nm) @ 3500rpm
Transmission	5-speed manual (3-speed auto in USA)	
Brakes	Vented disc/solid disc	Vented disc/solid disc
Length/Width/Height	4295/1690/1265mm	4295/1690/1265mm
Weight	1190kg	1250kg

PERFORMANCE

Max speed (mph)	134	142 (later 150)
0-60mph (secs)	8.5	7.0 (later 6.7)
Fuel economy (mpg)	32.3	20
Desirability	***	
Availability	***	
Tuneability	***	

MAZDA RX-7 GENERATION II 1985-1991

The handling was keen but it was rather let down by non-responsive and over-light steering. Other weak points included a fidgety ride, poor fuel consumption and a lack of low-down torque. It was however very well-equipped.

In 1987 the RX-7 got a convertible body option, which was novel: at the time, no other mass-produced sports car apart from the Alfa Romeo Spider was available with a soft top. The roof could be arranged in three positions: open, closed or targa-style. While the coupé was a nominal 2+2, the convertible was a strict two-seater.

In 1989 a 15PS power hike brought the 1989 Turbo II almost to the supercar club – and European buyers at last got the Turbo as well, in coupé and plush power-roof cabriolet forms. The Generation II lasted until 1991. As ever, rotary engine problems mean big bills so get an expert to check any potential purchase over.

Rotary engine of up to 185PS and rear-wheel drive made this an exciting sports car.

Convertible body style arrived in 1987.

MAZDA RX-7
GENERATION III 1991-2002

Third-generation RX-7 knocked on the door of the supercar club.

If the second generation RX-7 Turbo II had started to knock on the supercar club door, the all-new Generation III RX-7 to which it passed the baton charged unashamedly into the supercar fold. Compact dimensions, a twin-turbo engine and relatively light weight all led to one conclusion – a very rapid form of transport.

It was launched in Japan at the 1991 Tokyo Motor Show with Anfini badging (Mazda's short-lived up-market domestic brand). Few people disagreed that the new RX-7 was beautifully styled with lithe curves and even a subtle double-bubble roof. The bodywork used much aluminium and thermoplastics to keep weight down to 1230kg.

European cars all had 240PS from the twin turbocharged 13B engine and achieved 156mph and 0-60mph in 6.0 seconds. In Japan the story was different. For starters the engine was tuned as high as 280PS and was capable of 0-60mph in five seconds flat. Going in the opposite direction, a Touring version was available with a four-speed automatic transmission in Japan.

MAZDA RX-7 GENERATION III 1991-2002

This was now a highly sophisticated piece of performance engineering.

Interior reflected 1990s advances in equipment and design.

MAZDA RX-7 GENERATION III 1991-2002

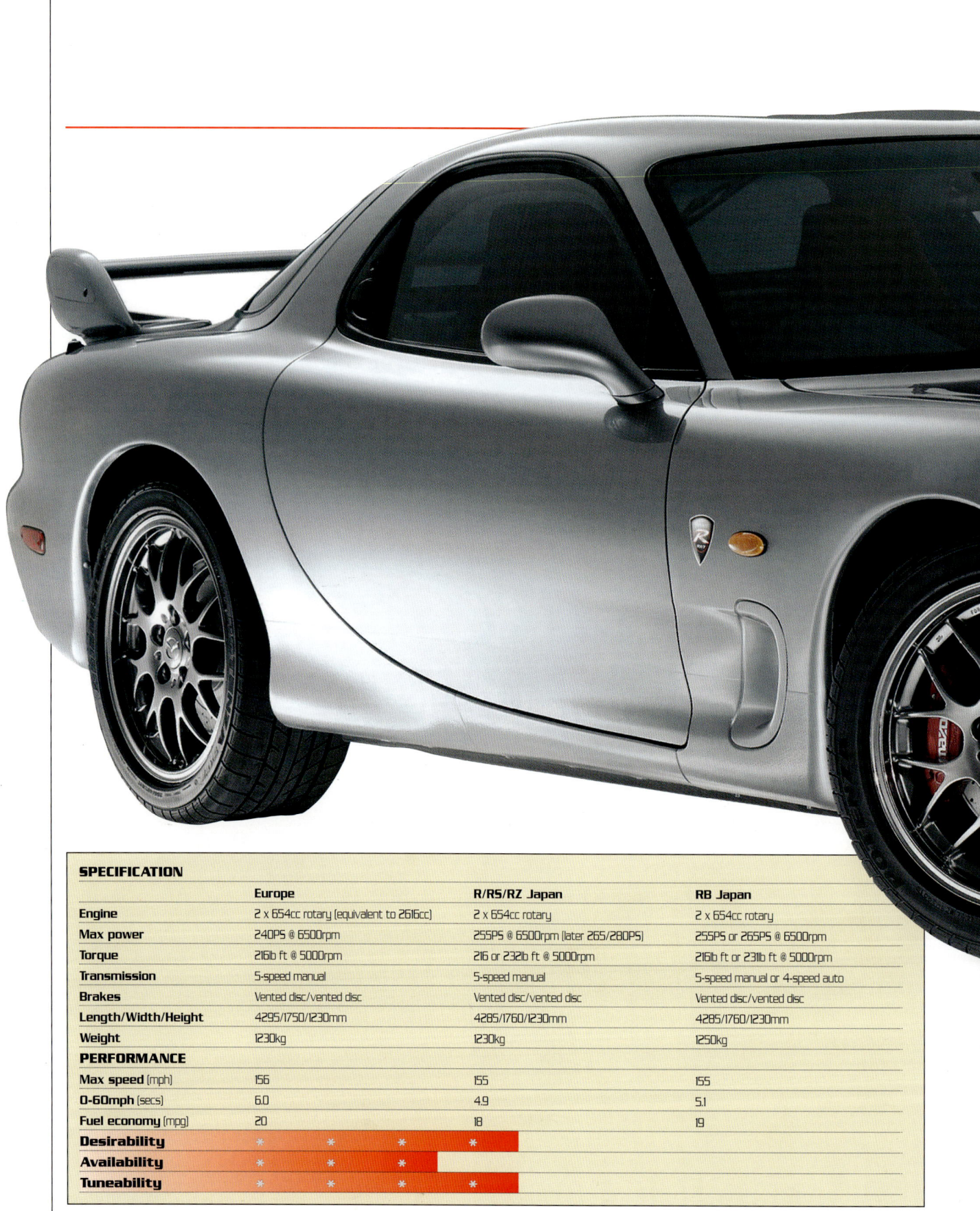

SPECIFICATION

	Europe	R/RS/RZ Japan	RB Japan
Engine	2 x 654cc rotary (equivalent to 2616cc)	2 x 654cc rotary	2 x 654cc rotary
Max power	240PS @ 6500rpm	255PS @ 6500rpm (later 265/280PS)	255PS or 265PS @ 6500rpm
Torque	216lb ft @ 5000rpm	216 or 232lb ft @ 5000rpm	216lb ft or 231lb ft @ 5000rpm
Transmission	5-speed manual	5-speed manual	5-speed manual or 4-speed auto
Brakes	Vented disc/vented disc	Vented disc/vented disc	Vented disc/vented disc
Length/Width/Height	4295/1750/1230mm	4285/1760/1230mm	4285/1760/1230mm
Weight	1230kg	1230kg	1250kg

PERFORMANCE

Max speed (mph)	156	155	155
0-60mph (secs)	6.0	4.9	5.1
Fuel economy (mpg)	20	18	19
Desirability	★★★★		
Availability	★★★		
Tuneability	★★★★		

MAZDA RX-7 GENERATION III 1991-2002

MkIII RX-7 Type R Bathurst.

Later RX-7s became more extreme: this is a 2002 Spirit R.

Superlative handling, grip and poise combined with a raw sports car feel that marked a return to the philosophy of the first series. But this was certainly not an under-equipped car, boasting air conditioning, an electric sunroof and leather upholstery.

While it was a great sports car, the third generation RX-7 was ultimately the polar opposite of a popular sports car. Its appeal was to the refined palate – and the well-heeled, as it was priced at £32,535 in the UK, where it was quietly dropped in 1995 (after just 124 official sales). In 1995 there was a restyling job front and rear and in the cabin. The RX-7 left all other markets in 1997, save Japan where it continued until 2002 (with another facelift for 1999).

You need to be absolutely sure that the proper servicing has been carried out. High mileage engines may need expensive work, and values tend to crash for leggy cars. The RX-7 devours tyres (front and rear), as well as brake pads and discs. Some parts, such as the exhaust, are very costly to replace so it's wise to get someone who knows the cars to check things over thoroughly.

MAZDA
RX-8
2003-date

2003's RX-8 marked another innovatory milestone for Mazda.

Each evolution in Mazda's rotary sports car development has represented a major shift. The early RX-7 was a raw sports car, the Generation II was a bigger Porsche 944 rival, and the Generation III was a virtual supercar. With the RX-8 – first seen in 2002 but not productionised until April 2003 – Mazda changed tack again and created an utterly unique vehicle.

The RX-8 was effectively a four-door sports car. It retained its rotary engine but in an all-new development called Renesis. It also looked sensational and was priced well below rivals such as the Nissan 350Z.

At the heart of it all was the new Renesis 13B-MSP rotary engine. A twin-rotor unit of the same capacity as before (1308cc), it was now naturally aspirated yet was capable of up to 250PS – almost 200PS per litre without a turbo in sight! It employed side intake and exhaust ports and featured approximately 30% more intake area than previous rotary engines. Turbine-

MAZDA RX-8 2003-DATE

Getting rid of the B-pillar allowed unimpeded access for four people.

smooth, it offered decent performance, if not to the level of the purer RX-7.

A very competent chassis featured multi-link rear suspension and perfect 50/50 weight distribution because the compact engine was sited so far back. That engendered neutral-to-understeer handling characteristics, helped by electronic power-assisted steering.

The RX-8 was a striking car to look at too. The rear pair of the "Freestyle" four-door system opened from the C-pillar. There was no B-pillar at all, allowing decent access for four adults. The interior, too, looked very sporty, with combined analogue and digital instrumentation and a rotary-triangle theme throughout.

In the UK, two versions were marketed: one with 192PS and one with 231PS. Both got a CD player, 18-inch alloys, traction control and climate control, while the 231PS model added Xenon headlights, a six-speed gearbox and an alloy pedal set.

In Japan, there were also two RX-8 versions but both had more power: the base model had 210PS and a five-speed gearbox (or four-speed auto option), while the more powerful Type S model had 250PS and a six-speed gearbox. In 2004, Mazda launched a limited-edition Mazdaspeed Version with a tuned engine, tweaked suspension and aero body parts. 300 were made in February 2004, followed later by 180 Mazdaspeed Version II units.

The press raved about the RX-8 and order books bulged. It may not have had the raw edge of the Nissan 350Z or the old RX-7 but it was attractive, refined, practical and had that certain must-have factor. The majority of owners went for the higher-powered model and usually added leather trim. Early reliability reports have been favourable but heavy fuel consumption is matched by heavy oil consumption, requiring frequent checks.

Renesis rotary engine was offered in two states of tune.

SPECIFICATION	192PS Europe	231PS Europe	RX-8 & Type E Japan	Type S Japan
Engine	2 x 654cc rotary	2 x 654cc rotary	2 x 654cc rotary	2 x 654cc rotary
Max power	192PS @ 7000rpm	231PS @ 8200rpm	210PS @ 7200rpm	250PS @ 8500rpm
Torque	162lb ft (220Nm) @ 5000rpm	155lb ft (211Nm) @ 5000rpm	163lb ft (221Nm) @ 5000rpm	159lb ft (216Nm) @ 5500rpm
Transmission	5-speed manual	6-speed manual	5-sp man or 4-sp auto	6-speed manual
Brakes	Vented disc/vented disc	Vented disc/vented disc	Vented disc/vented disc	Vented disc/vented disc
Length/Width/Height	4430/1770/1340mm	4430/1770/1340mm	4430/1770/1340mm	4430/1770/1340mm
Weight	1345kg	1345kg	1350kg	1350kg
PERFORMANCE				
Max speed (mph)	139	146	140	155
0-60mph (secs)	7.6	6.2	6.8	6.0
Fuel economy (mpg)	26	25	25	23
Desirability	*	*	*	*
Availability	*	*	*	* *
Tuneability	*	*	*	*

MAZDA
6 MPS

2005-date

The four-door body was stiffened by 40 per cent.

Pundits were agreed that the Mazda6 boasted one of the best chassis of any medium-sized family car. So Mazda decided to create a rival for the Subaru Impreza and Mitsubishi Evo, launching the Mazda6 MPS in 2005.

A turbocharged, direct injection version of Mazda's four-cylinder 2.3-litre engine produced 260PS at 6000rpm, with a higher torque output than the Impreza or Evo (280lb ft at 3000rpm). The Japanese version, known as Mazdasport Atenza, produced slightly more power with a claimed 272PS.

A new six-speed gearbox was not really close-ratio (sixth was an overdrive) which left the MPS trailing in the 0-60mph contest (6.6 secs).

A new Active Torque Split four-wheel drive system tracked steering angle, yaw rate, lateral g-force and engine status to determine road surface and driving conditions, then adjusted front/rear wheel torque distribution. Under normal conditions, it was front-wheel drive, moving to 50:50 when conditions dictated. Like the Evo, there were three modes (Normal, Sports and Snow) but these were not manually selectable. There was however a Power Take Off launch control system.

The four-door saloon body was stiffened by 40 per cent, while the suspension got uprated dampers and stiffer springs. Enormous 17-inch brake discs worked with ABS, brake assist, Dynamic Stability Control and the Active Torque Split 4x4 system.

As for looks, the bonnet had a good old-fashioned bulge, there were new bumpers, a rear spoiler, side skirts and wheelarches to cover 18-inch alloys shod with 215/45 tyres.

MAZDA 6 MPS 2005-DATE

The Mazda6 MPS was built to compete with the Subaru Impreza and Mitsubishi Evo.

The MPS features a sombre but sporting interior.

SPECIFICATION	
Engine	2261cc 4-cy
Max power	260PS @ 6000rpm
Torque	280lb ft (380Nm) at 3000rpm
Transmission	6-speed manual
Brakes	Vented disc/vented disc
Length/Width/Height	4740/1780/1445mm
Weight	n/a
PERFORMANCE	
Max speed (mph)	150
0-60mph (secs)	6.6
Fuel economy (mpg)	25
Desirability	* * *
Availability	* * * *
Tuneability	* * *

MAZDA

Other models

Most of us have heard of Mazda's twin-rotary engined RX-7. But mention the name Cosmo and you'll get a more quizzical look. The Cosmo badge was first created in 1967 when, historically, Mazda launched the world's first-ever twin-rotary car with the **Cosmo 110S**. This was an intriguing car in virtually every respect: great-looking, technically fascinating, powerful (128bhp and 125mph) but thirsty and unreliable.

Mazda continued to offer rotary-powered Cosmo coupés throughout the 1970s and 1980s but one stands out: the 1990 **Eunos Cosmo**. This elegantly-styled four-seater coupé was produced in limited series until 1995. The Type S had a twin-rotor engine but the Type E boasted no less than three rotors and was the world's first series production engine with twin sequential turbochargers. Over 390Nm of torque was available from as little as 2200rpm, while the 280PS power output was probably actually well in excess of 300PS.

Mazda's only other interesting sporty car was the curious little **Autozam AZ-1**. This tiny two-seater mid-engined sports car conformed to Japan's K-car city car rules, which meant a 64PS three-cylinder engine and minute dimensions. Its construction was novel: a space-frame with non-stressed glassfibre panels that could be readily removed (exploiting this, several special bodied models were made). The AZ-1's party piece was, however, its novel gullwing door arrangement. They're extremely rare and sought-after in Japan but it's worth tracking one down as the handling is so sharp.

Launched in 1968, the Cosmo Sport 110S had the world's first twin-rotor engine.

Wacky Autozam AZ-1 had plastic bodywork and gullwing doors.

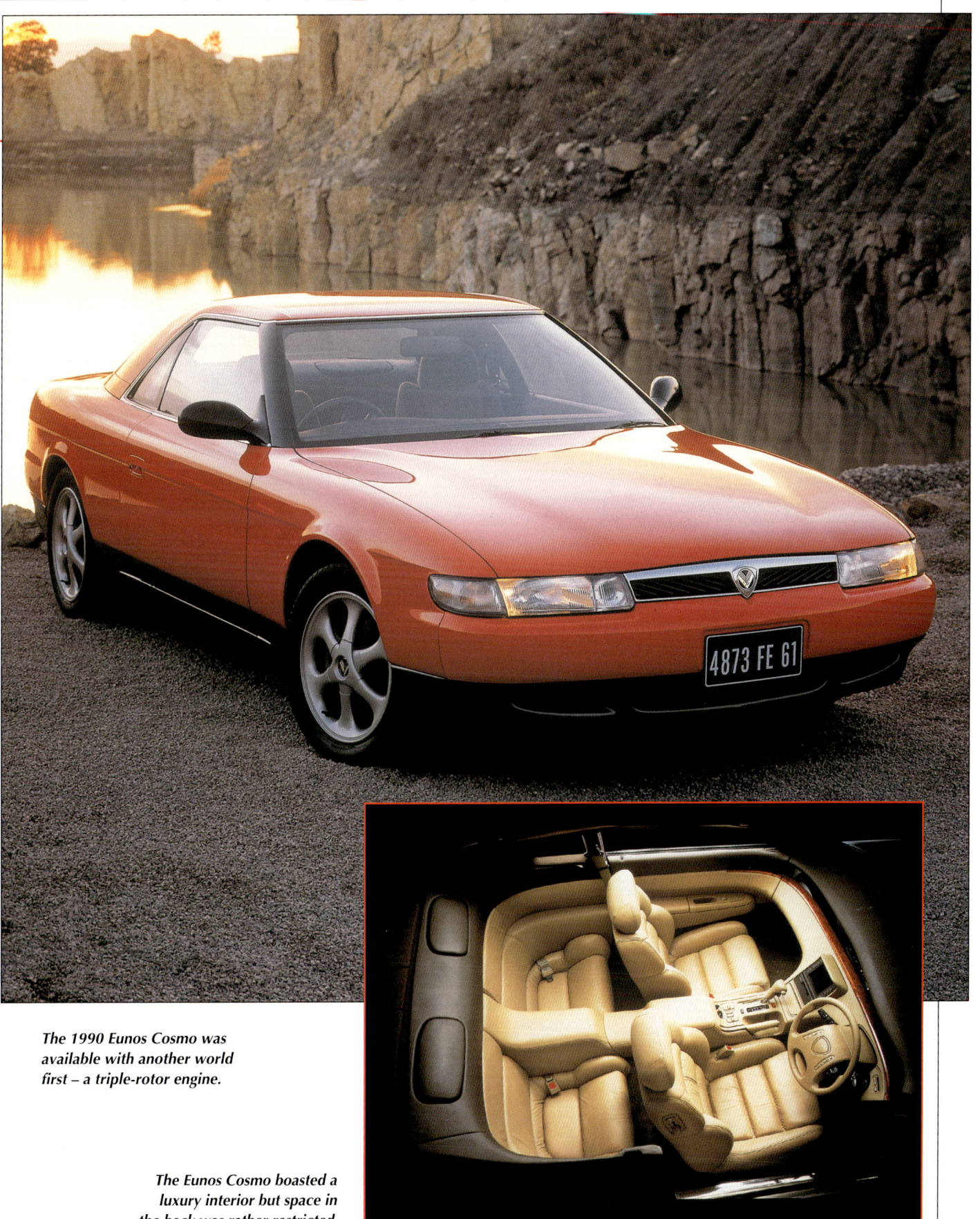

The 1990 Eunos Cosmo was available with another world first – a triple-rotor engine.

The Eunos Cosmo boasted a luxury interior but space in the back was rather restricted.

MITSUBISHI COLT

GTI 1992-1995

Fairly restrained looks for the 1992 Mitsubishi Colt GTi.

SPECIFICATION	
Engine	1834cc 4-cyl
Max power	140PS @ 6500rpm
Torque	123lb ft (167Nm) @ 5500rpm
Transmission	5-speed manual
Brakes	Vented disc/solid disc
Length/Width/Height	3870/1680/1385mm
Weight	995kg
PERFORMANCE	
Max speed (mph)	130
0-60mph (secs)	7.4
Fuel economy (mpg)	37
Desirability	✱ ✱
Availability	✱ ✱
Tuneability	✱ ✱ ✱

While most enthusiast interest surrounds the Japanese-market Mirage Cyborg R, Mitsubishi did market a 'warm' version of this car in Europe under the Colt GTI badge.

The early shape incarnation (1988-1991) came with a non-turbo 125PS 1.6-litre 16-valve engine, later switched to the 1834cc 4G93 16-valve four-cylinder engine with 136PS. In its later (1992-1995) version the 1.8 engine went up to 140PS. That was enough for a 0-60mph time of 7.4 seconds, making it a respectable GTI.

Shame both generations of Colt looked so dowdy, despite their roof spoilers. Despite the '92-'95 model sharing some of its underpinnings with the earliest Lancer, the front-drive Colt was no Evo to drive: it was competent rather than exciting.

It's reasonably cheap to run (low insurance, decent economy) and reliable with it. A very similar car is still made in Malaysia as the Proton Satria GTI.

MITSUBISHI MIRAGE
Cyborg & VR-X 1992-2000

Mitsubishi Mirage Cyborg R was a Japanese icon boasting 175PS.

The Japanese market Mirage Cyborg RS was down-specced and used steel wheels.

Cyborg sounds like something that's escaped from a Japanese sci-fi B-movie – and in the case of the Mirage Cyborg, that's not too far wrong. Based on the rather staid Mirage (sold as the Colt in most export markets), it is a little-known performance jewel.

The secret to the Mirage Cyborg was its 4G92 1.6-litre engine with a MIVEC head (variable valve timing and electronic valve lift). Producing 175PS from only 1.6 litres is a feat in itself, and it revved to 8200rpm. The Cyborg had harder suspension, a close-ratio five-speed gearbox and 15-inch alloy wheels with 195/55 tyres. Externally, a rear roof spoiler on the three-door hatchback was an easy identifier (there was also an Asti version of the Cyborg – basically a Mirage with a boot).

A basic, plasticky interior with very little sound-proofing was alleviated somewhat by Recaro seats and a Momo steering wheel, plus standard climate control.

Despite its great-looking spec and pace, the Cyborg never had the cachet of a Pulsar GTI-R or Integra Type R (it was targeted more at the Honda Civic SiR). Compared to many Japanese performance icons, its handling was not in the same league, it was down on power and it didn't have the right badge.

There are two generations to discover: the CA4A Cyborg R (1992-1994) and the CJ4A Cyborg ZR (1995-2000). In the UK there was little interest in the car, even through Mitsubishi's "official" grey importer, Ralliart. There was also a non-Cyborg Mirage VR-X, sometimes described as a "junior Evo" because it has 4x4. It has a larger 4G93 1.8-litre engine with 205PS but is heavier – and should not be confused with an Australian market Mirage VR-X which was a simple, boring dress-up limited edition.

SPECIFICATION		
	VR-X	Cyborg ZR
Engine	1834cc 4-cyl	1597cc 4-cyl
Max power	205PS @ 6000rpm	175PS @ 7500rpm
Torque	202lb ft (275Nm) @ 3000rpm	123lb ft (167Nm) @ 7000rpm
Transmission	5-speed manual	5-speed manual
Brakes	Vented disc/solid disc	Vented disc/solid disc
Length/Width/Height	3870/1680/1385mm	3870/1680/1385mm
Weight	1240kg	1070kg
PERFORMANCE		
Max speed (mph)	137	127
0-60mph (secs)	6.8	6.8
Fuel economy (mpg)	28	30
Desirability	★ ★	
Availability	★	
Tuneability	★ ★ ★	

MITSUBISHI COLT

CZT 2005-date

Producing 150PS from its 1.5-litre turbocharged MIVEC engine, the CZT was capable of 0-60mph in 8.0 seconds.

The Mitsubishi Colt CZT was styled in Germany.

In 2005, Mitsubishi decided to bring some of the kudos of its Evo to the diminutive Colt, developed and produced alongside the Smart forfour. The Colt CZT had a promising spec sheet.

Its specially-developed 1.5-litre MIVEC engine featured an intercooled turbo and variable valve timing. The engine also boasted hollow camshafts and low-friction pistons enabling it to reach a healthy 150PS. In action, the engine didn't sound anything special and needed to be revved hard to get the best out of it, when it became rather raucous. Transmitting its power through a Getrag five-speed gearbox, the CZT was lukewarm with 0-62mph time in 8.0 seconds and a top speed of 130mph.

The CZT (three-door only) got a reinforced bodyshell with front strut brace, stiffer springs, stronger stabiliser bar mounting, reinforced rear suspension arms, quick-rack steering, traction control/ESP, 15-inch ventilated front discs and wide 205-section tyres on 16-inch alloys. That was a recipe for a very grippy chassis, plus a welcome absence of torque steer and pleasingly direct steering. The ESP system cut in early though, keeping things safe rather than fun.

The CZT was styled in Germany to appeal to European tastes: a chunky front bumper with mesh grilling, side air dams, a tiny rear spoiler, dark grey headlamp bezels, colour-keyed trim and a large-bore exhaust tailpipe. Inside you got sports seats, white dials, silver trim accents, red-and-black leather steering wheel with radio controls, leather gear knob, sports seats and drilled aluminium pedals.

SPECIFICATION

Engine	1499cc 4-cyl
Max power	150PS @ 6000rpm
Torque	155lb ft (210Nm) @ 3500rpm
Transmission	5-speed manual
Brakes	Disc/disc
Length/Width/Height	3870/1695/1550mm
Weight	960kg

PERFORMANCE

Max speed (mph)	130
0-60mph (secs)	8.0
Fuel economy (mpg)	41
Desirability	★★★
Availability	★★★★
Tuneability	★★

A sports interior completed the package.

MITSUBISHI STARION

1982-1990

The original 2.0-litre turbo engine produced 170PS – 15bhp more than the later naturally aspirated 2.6-litre engine. This an earlier narrow-bodied version.

This is the wide-bodied version of Mitsubishi Starion launched in 1986 (1989 in the UK).

The myth goes that the Japanese linguistic mix-up between "r" and "l" led to a stallion becoming a malapropism. Whether that's true or not, Mitsubishi's Starion was certainly a feisty turbo coupé with a dash of the raw mustang about it.

Its rear-wheel drive handling was lairy, especially when the turbo boost cut-in as you exited a bend. Initially the Starion used the familiar 4G63 2.0-litre in-line four with a single turbo, kicking out 170PS in European spec but up to 197PS in Japan (which had three valves per cylinder and charge cooling).

A wide-bodied model became the export version from 1986 (1989 in the UK), whose flared arches covered wider tracks front and rear for more assured handling. The engine was expanded to a 2.6-litre in-line four at the same time (less power but more torque).

There was always decent grunt but image-wise the Starion strayed too far into Ford Capri territory. The Starion still has its followers but they have to put up with rampaging rust problems and the need to sport an '80s hairdo.

SPECIFICATION	2000	2600
Engine	1997cc 4-cyl	2555cc 4-cyl
Max power	170PS @ 5500rpm	155PS @ 5000rpm
Torque	181lb ft (245Nm) @ 3500rpm	210lb ft (284Nm) @ 2500rpm
Transmission	5-sp man or 4-sp auto	5-sp man or 4-sp auto
Brakes	Vented disc/vented disc	Vented disc/vented disc
Length/Width/Height	4425/1705/1315mm	4425/1745/1315mm
Weight	1250kg	1320kg
PERFORMANCE		
Max speed (mph)	137	134
0-60mph (secs)	7.4	7.8
Fuel economy (mpg)	28	26
Desirability	* *	
Availability	* *	
Tuneability	* * *	

The Starion proved to be a capable racing car.

MITSUBISHI ECLIPSE

1989-date

Strictly speaking, the Mitsubishi Eclipse is not a Japanese performance car at all, since it was designed and built in the USA. Chrysler set up Diamond Star Motors in Normal, Illinois to build the 2+2 coupé, which was also sold as the Plymouth Laser and Eagle Talon. From launch in 1989 the Eclipse was also sold in Japan as an import model and even made it to some European markets – but not the UK as it was only ever left-hand drive.

In technical terms, the Eclipse was based on the contemporary Galant. The range began with a lame 1.8 model (93PS), through a 140PS 2.0 twin cam, up to a 200PS 2.0 Turbo version – a genuinely quick car. The Turbo was sold in the USA, as were the lesser versions, with front-wheel drive, but the permanent four-wheel drive Turbo was the one to have.

After a minor facelift in 1992, the Eclipse got a full redesign in 1994. All models now had a 2.0-litre engine, the turbo models rising to 210PS. In 1995 a convertible body style was added, known as the Spyder, and at the same time a naturally aspirated 2.4-litre engine was added.

An all-new Eclipse arrived in 2000. Gone were the less and less popular turbo engines and all-wheel drive in favour of a 2.4-litre four-cylinder engine or a 3.0-litre V6. The new Eclipse was substantially larger, with a longer wheelbase and overall length and more interior space. A year later the Spyder convertible body style was revived. All versions of the Eclipse are a rare sight outside the USA.

Mitsubishi's Eclipse (here in 1993) was actually built in the USA.

MITSUBISHI ECLIPSE 1989-DATE

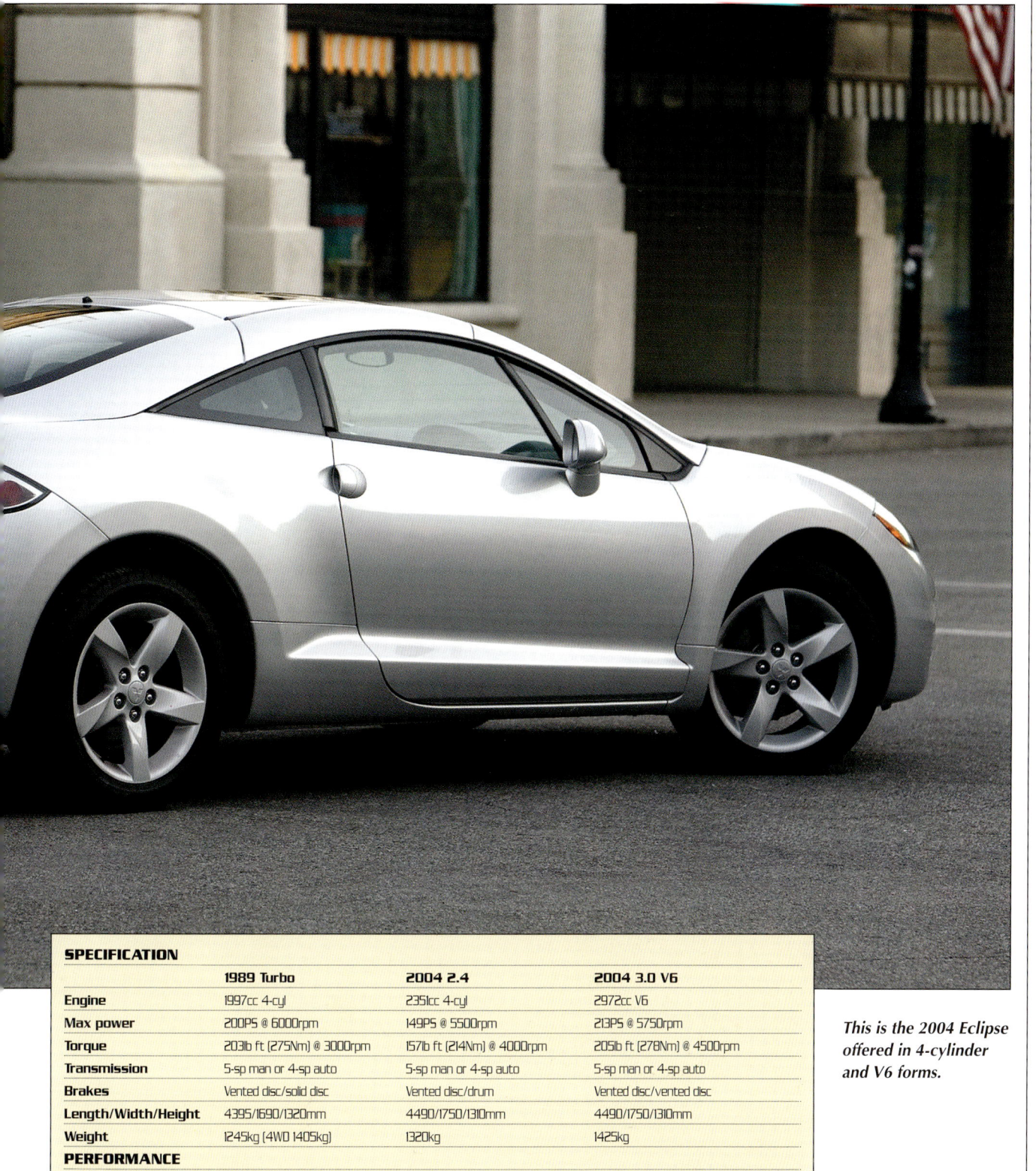

This is the 2004 Eclipse offered in 4-cylinder and V6 forms.

SPECIFICATION	1989 Turbo	2004 2.4	2004 3.0 V6
Engine	1997cc 4-cyl	2351cc 4-cyl	2972cc V6
Max power	200PS @ 6000rpm	149PS @ 5500rpm	213PS @ 5750rpm
Torque	203lb ft (275Nm) @ 3000rpm	157lb ft (214Nm) @ 4000rpm	205lb ft (278Nm) @ 4500rpm
Transmission	5-sp man or 4-sp auto	5-sp man or 4-sp auto	5-sp man or 4-sp auto
Brakes	Vented disc/solid disc	Vented disc/drum	Vented disc/vented disc
Length/Width/Height	4395/1690/1320mm	4490/1750/1310mm	4490/1750/1310mm
Weight	1245kg (4WD 1405kg)	1320kg	1425kg
PERFORMANCE			
Max speed (mph)	143	130	136
0-60mph (secs)	6.3	8.2	6.5
Fuel economy (mpg)	25	28	24
Desirability	*	*	*
Availability	*	*	
Tuneability	*	*	*

Second-generation Eclipse grew in size.

MITSUBISHI FTO
1994-2000

The naturally-aspirated 2.0-litre V6 MIVEC engine gave 200PS at a heady 7500rpm.

Mitsubishi's FTO (GPX pictured) was a remarkably accomplished mid-sized coupe.

It is not difficult to see why Mitsubishi's FTO coupé took off in the UK as one of the most successful grey imports of all time. Despite only ever being available as a grey import, its combination of great looks, raw talent and reasonable prices have endeared it to thousands of buyers.

The FTO was launched in 1994 and it immediately took the 1994/95 Japanese Car of the Year title – quite justifiably, for here was a car that was an easy match for the best European coupés.

At the heart of the FTO range lay a gem of a V6 twin cam engine with a system known as MIVEC. The MIVEC engine had two sets of cam lobes, one for low-down torque response and the other for top-end power. This provided silky-smooth cruising with a throaty surge of power when you revved the engine hard. And it could certainly rev freely – the MIVEC engine's power output of 200PS came at a scintillating 7500rpm.

The most popular transmission for the FTO was Mitsubishi's Tiptronic-style INVECS-II "intelligent" five-speed automatic. This normally operated in fully automatic mode, while a computer learnt the driver's personal driving style and adapted accordingly. It also recognised the difference between hills and flat roads. If you wanted more spirited performance, you could switch into Sports mode across the gate and operate the gearbox manually via a sequential up/down shift.

Features of the chassis included state-of-the-art MacPherson strut front and multilink rear suspension, all-round disc brakes (ventilated up front), ABS, twin anti-roll bars, optional traction control on the front-wheel drive and alloy wheels fitted with wide-section low-profile tyres. The handling was widely praised, while this was a remarkably grown-up car to drive too.

The interior was yet another FTO strong point. It had the usual Japanese features of excellent build quality and high equipment levels, but managed to look and feel more focused than the average dowdy-looking Japanese coupé. There was an angled centre console with hooded dials and clear instruments visible through the Momo leather-rim steering wheel. The rear seats were rather cramped, however.

To break down the different versions on offer, the FTO range was topped by the MIVEC-powered 200PS 2.0-litre GPX, which also featured uprated brakes and suspension compared to lesser FTOs. The same mechanical specification but extra performance could be had from the 30kg lighter GP Version R, which was also a little cheaper to buy. Stepping down the range came the GX and GR with a less powerful 170PS version of the 2.0-litre V6 engine (these could not be bought with the INVECS semi-auto). At the base of the range was an entry-level GS powered by a 125PS 1.8-litre four-cylinder unit that is best avoided.

The muscular styling of the FTO was updated in 1996, gaining a

FTO was imported by Ralliart into the UK.

deeper front air dam with a single air intake and circular cut-outs for the foglamps and indicators. An Aero Series body styling package was a popular option for the model's whole life, featuring a very large rear wing.

Some FTOs were brought into the UK by Ralliart but almost all were imported independently. The large numbers around mean that parts are not a problem but you should shop around before buying. Check your car has immaculate bodywork, proper servicing and does not suffer from worn brakes or tyres. If you're going for the INVECS gearbox, check it shifts smoothly and both automatic and manual functions work properly. Also the V6 engines are awkward to work on – even changing the spark plugs requires hours of labour time.

FTO had a better interior than many Japanese coupes and a semi-automatic gearbox option.

SPECIFICATION	GPX/GPR	GR/GX	GS
Engine	1999cc V6	1999cc V6	1834cc 4-cyl
Max power	200PS @ 7500rpm	170PS @ 7000rpm	125PS @ 6000rpm
Torque	147lb ft (200Nm) @ 6000rpm	137lb ft (186Nm) @ 4400rpm	119lb ft (162Nm) @ 4500rpm
Transmission	5-sp man or 5-sp auto	5-sp man or 4-sp auto	5-sp man or 4-sp auto
Brakes	Vented disc/solid disc	Vented disc/solid disc	Vented disc/solid disc
Length/Width/Height	4320/1735/1300mm	4320/1735/1300mm	4320/1735/1300mm
Weight	1210/1190kg	1150kg	1100kg
PERFORMANCE			
Max speed (mph)	142	136	125
0-60mph (secs)	7.0	7.9	9.2
Fuel economy (mpg)	22	23	27
Desirability	★ ★ ★ ★		
Availability	★ ★ ★ ★		
Tuneability	★ ★ ★		

MITSUBISHI GTO & 3000GT

1990-2000

With four-wheel drive, four-wheel steer and lots of electronic driver aids, the 3000GT was a strong performer.

In the US a Spyder version of the 3000GT was announced in 1994 with a retractable hardtop.

The 1990s saw an explosion of Japanese supercars such as the Nissan Fairlady/300ZX and Mazda RX-7. Somehow Mitsubishi's effort got lost in the flurry and has, perhaps unfairly, been a victim of a whispering campaign.

This car was known as the 3000GT in Europe, in Japan as the GTO and in America a version was marketed as the Dodge Stealth. Whatever it was called, it was a junior exotic bursting with technological fireworks. The most sophisticated versions had permanent four-wheel drive with a 45/55 front/rear torque split, four-wheel steering using same-phase technology and other whizzbangs including ABS, electronically-controlled dampers and cruise control.

As for the engine, this was a 3.0-litre 24-valve V6 with twin turbochargers, twin intercoolers, twin overhead camshafts and alloy cylinder heads. That let loose 286PS in European tune (280PS in Japan, 304PS in other markets). A more modest and far less exciting non-turbo version was also marketed with 225PS, but not in the UK, while there was also a two-wheel drive model for the USA.

While the GTO was astonishingly quick both in a straight line and around corners, it was often criticised for being uninvolving to drive – all those driver aids made you go quicker, but they took some of the fun out of the equation. But what that meant in practice was

This is the final GTO Mk3 1999 facelift, for Japan only.

that virtually anyone could drive a GTO blisteringly quickly in total safety.

The criticisms did not detract from the GTO's sheer road presence and seat-flattening performance, though. The interior was rakishly styled (looking much more purposeful than most Japanese cars) and lavishly equipped. The GTO could seat 2+2 people, while the hatchback tailgate offered a reasonable level of practicality.

Let's sort out the Japanese versions. First up is the 280PS Twin Turbo model, in two versions, one with four-wheel steering and another (the MR) which lacked all-wheel steering. An automatic transmission was available on the normally-aspirated 225PS SR, while post-1995 Twin-Turbo manual cars have six speeds. UK cars were always twin turbo, 4x4, manuals.

3000GT featured a gadget-laden and luxurious interior.

MITSUBISHI GTO & 3000GT 1990-2000

The GTO went through two major evolution phases. The first models (1990-93) had pop-up headlamps and a squarish front end, then from 1993 a new front end with twin fixed projector headlamps, new more curvaceous bonnet and new rear lights. The 1999 model GTO (UK imports stopped in 1999) gained another new front end treatment, with a larger front air intake and new lights.

You would be hard-pushed to find a more convincing junior supercar bargain than this. What to look out for? It's a complicated beast so check for engine management problems and turbo gremlins, the electric dampers, exhaust (very expensive), steering (also expensive) and that all the warning lights come on and then go off. The image is more grand tourer than out-and-out sports car, so tuning parts are not always easy to track down.

A 1993 facelift saw the pop-up headlights replaced with twin fixed projector headlamps.

SPECIFICATION	Europe	Japan Twin-Turbo	Japan Non-Turbo
Engine	2972cc V6	2972cc V6	2972cc V6
Max power	286PS @ 6000rpm	280PS @ 6000rpm	225PS @ 6000rpm
Torque	300lb ft (407Nm) @ 2500rpm	307lb ft (417Nm) @ 2500rpm	202lb ft (275Nm) @ 4500rpm
Transmission	5 or 6-speed manual	5 or 6-speed manual	5-speed manual or 4-speed auto
Brakes	Vented disc/vented disc	Vented disc/vented disc	Vented disc/vented disc
Length/Width/Height	4600/1840/1285mm	4600/1840/1285mm	4600/1840/1285mm
Weight	1680kg	1600kg	1600kg
PERFORMANCE			
Max speed (mph)	158	143	
0-60mph (secs)	5.6	6.7	
Fuel economy (mpg)	18	20	
Desirability	* * * *		
Availability	* * *		
Tuneability	* * * *		

MITSUBISHI LANCER
EVO I, II & III 1992-1996

1993 Lancer Evolution II had longer wheelbase, better suspension and more power.

Got caught up in the euphoria surrounding the Evo VI but can't afford to buy one? Well you could consider an earlier Evo model such as a I, II or III. They may not be the thrill of the moment, look as wild or go as fast, but they all offer the genuine Lancer Evo magic for a bargain price.

The origin of the celebrated Mitsubishi Lancer Evo series goes back to 1992, when Mitsubishi launched an Evolution version of the tame Lancer saloon. It got Mitsubishi's lightweight car homologated into rallying, although initially it was a quiet start. Only when the Evo won its first WRC event did the legend come to life.

Evo I
The early road Evo came in three generations, I, II and III. All shared a tenacious four-wheel drive chassis and a mighty 4G63 turbocharged 2.0-litre four-cylinder engine derived from the Galant VR-4. In its first incarnation, the Evolution had 250PS courtesy of an IHI turbocharger, twin cams and four valves per cylinder, plus lightened crankshaft, con rods and pistons. The gearbox was also taken from the VR-4 but with double-cone second gear synchro and a tougher clutch.

Externally, the Evo (which was a totally different car to the Lancer sold in Europe) gained a deep front spoiler with a central grille for the intercooler, louvres in the aluminium bonnet, fat 15-inch alloy wheels and 195/55 tyres and a workmanlike boot-mounted rear wing that reduced rear-end lift by 18%. No spotlamps, no fat wheelarches, no outrageous wings… yet.

Evo II
With the Evo II, which arrived at the end of 1993, power was boosted to 260PS as a result of uprating the turbo, reducing exhaust back-pressure and increasing valve lift. But most attention went on the handling, and the Evo II got a 10mm longer wheelbase, 5-10mm wider tracks, bigger OZ wheels and wider tyres, revised front suspension lower arms and struts, readjusted front camber and improved damping. Aerodynamically, an airdam under the front spoiler and a more effective rear spoiler improved air flow. That made it a faster and better-handling car, "especially on tarmac" said Mitsubishi. It was right: the Evo II scored the Lancer's first WRC victory on the 1995 Swedish Rally.

Evo III

When the Evo III arrived in early 1995, there were only a few changes, most of which concerned the aerodynamics: larger air ducts, extended front air dam, larger rear wing and new side skirts. The intercooler got a second water spray nozzle and the engine gained an extra 10PS, taking it to 270PS. The chassis was left unaltered.

The Evo was well into its stride in rallying by this stage, with Tommi Mäkinen winning the first of his WRC championships in 1996. The magic rubbed off on to the road car programme, but outside Japan Mitsubishi continued to sell cars only to serious rallying contenders.

Two versions of the Evo were always available: the well-equipped GSR and the stripped-out lightweight RS. The RS gives you the unyieldingly raw feel of a rally car and is often the model chosen if you're planning major tuning. However the GSR is much easier to live with on a day-to-day basis: less noise, more equipment. It's also worth mentioning that there were early 1.8-litre sub-Evo Lancer GSR and RS variations which only had 195-205PS – not proper Evos despite their large rear spoilers and turbo power.

The first Lancer Evolution arrived in 1992 to a relatively quiet reception.

Early Evos offer most of the thrills and roadkills of later examples but at a fraction of the cost. Performance is very much in the supercar league (0-60mph in five seconds flat), while the levels of grip on offer outclass just about everything else, at this price level at least.

Gearboxes can get very notchy and crunchy with age and rebuild costs are steep. You can extend transmission life by filling it with synthetic oil. Bushes are a common fail point but aren't expensive. Engines are very robust but listen for noisy tappets, fuel cuts and watch for a smoky exhaust. Front wings are easily dented too. Most cars on sale will have been modified in some way, as tuning is straightforward and uprating components is just as easy as replacing worn items. Parts used to be a problem for I, II and III cars but now there specialists around able to supply just about anything. Examples of the early Evo can now be picked up extremely cheaply – just don't expect running costs to be cheap (especially fuel and insurance).

1995 Evolution III marked some minor aerodynamic changes and a 270PS engine.

SPECIFICATION			
	Evo I	**Evo II**	**Evo III**
Engine	1997cc 4-cyl	1997cc 4-cyl	1997cc 4-cyl
Max power	250PS @ 6000rpm	260PS @ 6000rpm	270PS @ 6250rpm
Torque	230lb ft (313Nm) @ 3000rpm	228lb ft (309Nm) @ 3000rpm	228lb ft (309Nm) @ 3000rpm
Transmission	5-speed manual	5-speed manual	5-speed manual
Brakes	Vented disc/vented disc	Vented disc/vented disc	Vented disc/vented disc
Length/Width/Height	4310/1695/1420mm	4310/1695/1420mm	4310/1695/1395mm
Weight	1240kg (RS: 1170kg)	1250kg (RS: 1180kg)	1260kg (RS: 1190kg)
PERFORMANCE			
Max speed (mph)	140	140	140
0-60mph (secs)	5.2	5.1	5.0
Fuel economy (mpg)	22	21	20
Desirability	★ ★ ★ ★		
Availability	★ ★ ★		
Tuneability	★ ★ ★ ★ ★		

MITSUBISHI
LANCER
EVO IV, V & VI 1996-2001

Evo IV
What had started out as a rally homologation device quickly became a legend. A big leap forward arrived in August 1996 with the Evo IV, the first full model change in the Evo's development. Virtually every part of the car was changed and the Evo IV represented a huge evolution over the early Lancers.

Under the bonnet lay the same 4G63 engine but it now had lighter pistons, reprofiled cams, revised manifolds, a twin-scroll turbo, more boost pressure and a new intercooler to release 280PS and lots more torque. Also the engine (now with an evocative red cam cover) was rotated through 180 degrees to improve weight distribution and handling balance.

1996 saw the arrival of the all-new Lancer Evolution IV with its sensational active yaw control.

Perhaps the biggest news, however, was a world first on a production car: Mitsubishi's trademark Active Yaw Control (AYC). This actively controlled the torque delivered to the left and right wheels, adjusting the car's yaw moment to allow the tyres to perform to their maximum potential. This imbued the Evo IV with unbelievable cornering ability. The lightweight RS model had a helical limited slip diff instead of AYC – the first time a production car had been fitted with a front diff of this kind.

The Evo IV grew significantly in size with an all-new, aggressively styled body featuring a swoopy front air dam, massive spotlamps (blanks for the RS), bonnet louvres and an exotically-shaped rear spoiler. Weight was up on the Evo IV, too, but the advances elsewhere easily cancelled out the weight penalty. Indeed testers were bowled over by how much better the IV was than the III.

A much wider track (and wider body to suit) made the Evolution V an even sharper handler.

SPECIFICATION

	Evo IV	Evo V	Evo VI
Engine	1997cc 4-cyl	1997cc 4-cyl	1997cc 4-cyl
Max power	280PS @ 6500rpm	280PS @ 6500rpm	280PS @ 6500rpm
Torque	260lb ft (353Nm) @ 3000rpm	275lb ft (373Nm) @ 3000rpm	275lb ft (373Nm) @ 3000rpm
Transmission	5-speed manual	5-speed manual	5-speed manual
Brakes	Vented disc/vented disc	Vented disc/vented disc	Vented disc/vented disc
Length/Width/Height	4330/1690/1415mm	4350/1770/1415mm	4350/1770/1415mm
Weight	1350kg (RS: 1260kg)	1360kg (RS: 1260kg)	1360kg (RS: 1260kg)
PERFORMANCE			
Max speed (mph)	145	145	150
0-60mph (secs)	4.8	4.8	4.7
Fuel economy (mpg)	20	20	20
Desirability	★ ★ ★ ★ ★		
Availability	★ ★ ★ ★		
Tuneability	★ ★ ★ ★ ★		

Evo interiors were focused rather than plush – this is an Evo V.

Engine, suspension and body changes marked the 1999 Evo VI.

Evo V

If the Evo IV had been a revelation, in January 1998 the Evo V changed the rulebook again. Torque was boosted thanks to a larger turbo nozzle, although the power output remained the same. The radiator was bigger and cooling improved significantly. The brakes got a huge boost, with Brembo four-pot front calipers and two-pot rears. The differentials were changed and you got a water-spray to cool it all down, while the steering box was repositioned to benefit weight distribution.

Both front and rear tracks grew wider and, in combination with new 17-inch alloys, that meant fat new wheelarches, and a wider front bumper/spoiler with integrated outer aerodynamic "ears". The rear wing got reverse-angle pillars to hold an adjustable aluminium blade. Aluminium was also chosen for the front wings as well as the bonnet. The suspension was improved too, adding to the wider tracks with a new front camber adjuster, inverted struts, stiffer springs and dampers and longer suspension travel.

Evo VI

Regarded by many as the ultimate Evo incarnation is the legendary Evo VI. Launched in January 1999, it looked even more aggressive and handled even more sharply.

It certainly looked the part. Rally regulations dictated a smaller rear spoiler but Mitsubishi responded with a twin-wing spoiler that kept down-force hefty. Other changes included a heavily blistered front air dam with spotlamps further apart, larger intake area, offset front number plate and side oil cooler vents. A stiffer body helped its peerless handling.

Under the bonnet it gained a larger intercooler, oil cooler and radiator, better-cooled pistons plus a new ECU, while the lightweight RS got a titanium-aluminium alloy turbo (a world first) that sharpened throttle response.

Improvements in the suspension department included a repositioned ball joint to reduce roll centre

Special eXtreme model (Zero Fighter in Japan) had 340PS and a white-and-red colour scheme.

height, cast aluminium rear arms and longer rebound strokes. What was already legendary handling raised the game still further: the Evo VI was perhaps the best handling of any car in its day. This was also the first Evo to be imported officially to the UK, as Ralliart offered them initially, then Mitsubishi directly.

Evo VI Tommi Mäkinen

In 1999, Tommi Mäkinen won his fourth consecutive WRC driver's title in an Evo VI. What better way to celebrate this unprecedented achievement than to create a special edition Evo? And what an edition it was. The Tommi Mäkinen Edition (sometimes called TME or Evo 6.5) looked and felt like a rally car. The front end was remodelled with an oversize bumper, no spotlamps and an aggressive chin profile. The white 17-inch alloys were identical to Tommi's WRC car. Although available in silver, black, white and blue, red was the colour to have, complete with Ralliart rally graphics. Inside, there were Mäkinen-embroidered Recaros and a red colour scheme. Mechanically it got a titanium turbo, big exhaust, 10mm lower suspension, front strut bars and quicker steering.

This could very well be the ultimate Evo. It's based on the best Evo of all (the VI), it has an upgraded engine and chassis, rally-style interior and it looks just like Tommi Mäkinen's rally winner. Add to this the fact that only 2500 were built and you can see why owners are prepared to pay big premiums over the standard VI.

Evo extremes

Mitsubishi's racing wing Ralliart produced some special versions of the Evo V and VI. There was an RS II version of the Evo VI, which was essentially an RS with some GSR equipment added. Above this was the Evo VI RS Sprint, tuned by Ralliart to produce 320PS thanks to a special ECU, HKS exhaust and HKS air filter. The Evo VI RSX limited edition (30 built) was a sort of GSR/RS cross-over without AYC or ABS but with electric windows and mirrors, air con, quick steering rack and titanium turbo shaft and turbo wheel. It weighed 1280kg, significantly less than the GSR. There was also a special model called the Zero Fighter in Japan and eXtreme in the UK, which had 340PS and a white-and-red colour scheme with decals. The ultimate Evo VI was the RS450, based on the RS II to various specs but most commonly AP Racing brakes and a monster state of tune ("450" referred to the intended lb ft torque figure, but it was probably more like 390lb ft and 380PS in fact).

Look for

The addition of AYC means that if you hear a squawking sound from the rear diff area during cornering, this could indicate AYC problems – sometimes a flush through with fluid clears it, or the AYC ECU may be at fault. Check for front top suspension mount wear and that the Recaro seats' recline mechanism does not slip. Otherwise, the usual Evo issues apply (gearbox, bushes, panel damage). To buy, the Evo IV is underrated next to the V and VI, and has most of their go for a fraction of the cost. Clutches are weak if you do a lot of track days, but many cars have upgraded clutches now. Like all Evos, grey imports need to be checked thoroughly for rust, since they were not undersealed at the factory. A tappety sound usually indicates worn hydraulic lash adjusters but they're not expensive to fix.

As for the VI, UK cars are preferred (look for UK Ralliart service books, owners' manuals in English and a Thatcham Cat 1 alarm). Check for noisy rear differentials which can be costly to replace. Turbo noise and smoke could indicate bearing problems. Miles are less of an issue than service continuity (oil and timing belts especially). Looked after, the engine has a deserved bombproof reputation. Warped front discs are a well-known problem, fixable by fitting an aftermarket caliper and disc kit.

MITSUBISHI LANCER
EVO VII, VIII & IX 2001-date

In Japan, there was always a stripped-out RS version of every Evo generation.

SPECIFICATION	Evo VII	Evo VII FQ-300
Engine	1997cc 4-cyl	1997cc 4-cyl
Max power	280PS @ 6500rpm	309PS @ 6500rpm
Torque	282lb ft (353Nm) @3000rpm (GT-A 253lb ft)	300lb ft (407Nm) @ 4500rpm
Transmission	5-sp man/5-sp auto	5-sp man
Brakes	Vented disc/solid disc	Vented disc/vented disc
Length/Width/Height	4455/1770/1450mm	4455/1770/1450mm
Weight	1380kg (RS: 1320kg, GT-A 1480kg)	1380kg
PERFORMANCE		
Max speed (mph)	150	155
0-60mph (secs)	5.0	4.8
Fuel economy (mpg)	22	21
Desirability	★ ★ ★ ★ ★	
Availability	★ ★ ★ ★	
Tuneability	★ ★ ★ ★ ★	

Evo VII

If the Evo IV-VI was the Evo going lairy, the all-new 2001 Evo VII edged towards being sensible. It was a lot bigger (especially inside), 40kg heavier and toned down in style to the point of looking a little humdrum. Initially it looked a bit soft against the Evo VI, and perhaps Mitsubishi recognised this, for the Evo VII was priced lower than the outgoing VI.

The bodyshell was all-new, based on the Japanese market Cedia (thank Godzilla Mitsubishi did not call it the "seedier evolution"), and certainly quite a bit bigger. The wheelbase grew by 115mm, the front track is 5mm broader, the rear track 10mm. Despite the growth spurt, the shell was actually lighter (thanks to more use of aluminium) and stronger. Changes under the skin raised overall weight but only by 40kg to 1400kg. The big rear wing was nowhere near as outrageous as the wild double-pylon thing of the VI, while

The Evo VII was a much larger and more refined car than the Evo VI.

dinner-plate spotlamps were banished – the fogs were now incorporated into the headlamps.

The engine evolved only slightly: a more efficient turbo, enhanced exhaust and better cooling boosted torque, while a smaller turbine nozzle improved mid-range acceleration and response. The larger intercooler now had three spray nozzles rather than two, and an automatic spray mode was added. Lighter hollow camshafts permitted the engine to rev more freely and the exhaust was improved. The existing five-speed 'box was toughened up and the ratios widened.

But easily the most important improvement was a new Active Centre Differential (ACD), which worked alongside the existing Active Yaw Control (AYC). Replacing the Evo VI's mechanical centre viscous coupling, it used an electronically controlled multiple-plate clutch to improve response and reduce clutch slippage. In the instrument binnacle was an indicator letting you know which of three settings you have selected: tarmac, gravel or snow. Not often used but it impresses your mates.

The suspension was not radically altered, although the suspension arms were reinforced, there was a higher roll centre and wider wheels and tyres helped grip and high speed stability. The steering rack was mounted lower and the number of turns lock-to-lock reduced to only 2.0.

There was a big difference inside. The initial feeling of a disappointingly down-market cabin was alleviated by a Momo steering wheel and Recaro seats, while interior space was much improved, especially in the rear.

Japanese versions came in various forms: GSR, lightweight RS and, bizarrely, a lower-powered GT-A version with INVECS II five-speed semi-automatic transmission (what were they thinking?).

In the UK, an FQ-300 version was also offered from launch (2001). Mitsubishi claimed limply: "FQ could stand for 'flipping quick' – or 'fine quality' – your choice." Power went up to 309PS and torque rose 8.4% to 300lb ft. All for only £1500 extra. Xtreme Autos (formerly Ralliart UK) built the RS Sprint, with a mild hike in power (320PS) and torque thanks to increased boost and an improved induction kit.

UK cars are common and may have some warranty left (3 years, unlimited miles). Ensure you have a full service history. Plenty of grey imports around (pay less for these) which need special care. Check the clutch, body panels, differential, suspension bushes and tyres. By the way, avoid the import-only GT-A but the RS is worth a look: there is less to go wrong (no AYC fluid to change and no ABS).

Evo VIII

The Evo VIII arrived in January 2003. In Japan, three versions were available: the GSR with a new six-speed gearbox to match rival Subaru's Impreza STi; an RS with a new close-ratio five-speed gearbox; and an RS with the new six-speed 'box.

The 4G63 engine now offered more torque (392Nm) thanks to better turbocharging, while cooling was improved and uprated aluminium pistons and forged steel con rods were fitted. Lighter valve springs and tensioners reduced friction. Fuel tank capacity rose by 7 litres to 55, but this was still woefully small for a car of this thirst.

AYC evolved into "Super AYC" using a planetary gear differential in place of the bevel gear type in the previous AYC to double the amount of torque it can transfer between the rear wheels. The RS continued with ACD only (no AYC).

Externally, the Evo VIII got a more aggressive front grille and a slimmer, carbon fibre-reinforced plastic rear spoiler. Intercooler efficiency was boosted by an enlarged bumper air intake and the undertray was more aerodynamic. The body was also lighter and stiffer which, combined with minor suspension tweaks, sharpened the handling. New Enkei six-spoke 17-inch alloy wheels looked better too.

Inside there was new dark titanium trim plus blue inset panels, a revised gear lever, new dials and blue-finish Recaro seats.

The UK-only FQ-300 version kept the same 309PS engine as the VII version and UK customers took to it in their droves. An FQ-330 model from October 2003 delivered a mighty 335PS courtesy of a supplementary ECU controlling ignition timing and air/fuel mixture,

In the UK, FQ versions added extra power to the equation – particularly the FQ-300.

More torque, better AYC and a lighter body greeted the Evo VIII. This is the EU-spec Evo VIII 260.

plus increased turbo boost. The FQ-330 got black Alcantara leather seats and sat nav, and cars were individually numbered.

In October 2003 (2004 in Europe), a new Evo MR range was launched. MR stood for Mitsubishi Racing and denoted the fact that Mitsubishi had done it again – evolved the beast. The MR got an aluminium roof, Bilstein dampers, anthracite forged alloy wheels, lighter suspension, improved 4x4 and Super AYC, enhanced engine response, a tall carbon-fibre rear spoiler, carbon dash and special badging. Alongside the MR 280, FQ remained the uprated moniker in the UK – in FQ-300, FQ-320 and FQ-340 forms, the latter adding leather and sat nav.

The no-nonsense interior of the Evo VIII FQ-300.

The Evo VIII FQ-400 was a UK-edition model with no less than 410PS on tap.

Perhaps more significant was a new Evo VIII 260 designed for the European market. Detuned to 265PS, it was mated to a five- (not six-) speed gearbox yet lost very little in performance. It retained Super AYC, ABS and EBD, Recaro front seats and 17-inch alloy wheels – indeed the only exterior visual difference was a smaller rear spoiler.

In October 2004 Mitsubishi Motors UK unveiled "the fastest saloon car ever produced by a major manufacturer" – the MR FQ-400. That was no idle claim, as the new car hit 60mph in 3.8 seconds and reached a top speed of 175mph. Only 100 cars were to be made priced at £46,999. Most of the modification occurred under the bonnet: a Garrett GT turbocharger, stainless steel exhaust manifold, forged pistons and con rods, HKS injectors, steel head gasket, MoTeC ECU and iridium spark plugs. The net effect was 410PS and 355lb ft of torque. Braking was uprated with six-pot calipers, as was the clutch. Subtle bodywork changes included a striking "shark's tooth" rear vortex generator

SPECIFICATION				
	Evo VIII	Evo VIII 260	Evo VIII FQ-300	Evo VIII FQ-330
Engine	1997cc 4-cyl	1997cc 4-cyl	1997cc 4-cyl	1997cc 4-cyl
Max power	280PS @ 6500rpm	265PS @ 3600rpm	309PS @ 6200rpm	335PS @ 6800rpm
Torque	282lb ft (353Nm) @ 3000rpm	262lb ft (355Nm) @ 3500rpm	300lb ft (407Nm) @ 4500rpm	315lb ft (427Nm) @ 5000rpm
Transmission	6-sp manual	5-sp manual	6-sp manual	6-sp manual
Brakes	Vented disc/vented disc	Vented disc/vented disc	Vented disc/vented disc	Vented disc/vented disc
Length/Width/Height	4490/1770/1450mm	4490/1770/1450mm	4490/1770/1450mm	4490/1770/1450mm
Weight	1410kg (RS: 1320kg)	1470kg	1410kg	1410kg
PERFORMANCE				
Max speed (mph)	157	157	157	157
0-60mph (secs)	5.1	5.9	4.7	4.4
Fuel economy (mpg)	22	25	20	20
Desirability	★★★	★★★★	★★★★★	★★★★★
Availability	★★★	★★★	★★★★	★★★★
Tuneability	★★★	★★★	★★★★	★★★★★

MITSUBISHI LANCER EVO VII, VIII & IX 2001-DATE

The Evo VIII FQ-400 could hit 60mph in under four seconds.

above the rear window, Ralliart aero mirrors, carbon fibre front lip spoiler and gloss black alloy wheels.

When looking at a car to buy, most of the comments about the earlier Evos apply to the VII and VIII. Look for a slipping clutch, dented or stonechipped body panels, differential noises, worn bushes, even tyre wear and a clean, well looked-after interior. The FQ is a UK-only model with full dealer back-up. Ensure you have a full Mitsubishi service history and a clear HPI-type history check.

Mitsubishi Evo IX [2005-date]

Mitsubishi stuck resolutely to the 'if it ain't broke' formula with the 2005 launch of the Evo IX, leaving most of the Evo VIII MR spec well alone. The Evo IX was the most cautious and subtlest evolution yet: cosmetic tweaks and some engine changes – but that was about it.

The single most important change was the adoption of MIVEC – a clever variable valve timing system that matched the inlet valve timing according to engine

SPECIFICATION			
	Evo VIII MR FQ-320	Evo VIII MR FQ-340	Evo VIII MR FQ-400
Engine	1997cc 4-cyl	1997cc 4-cyl	1997cc 4-cyl
Max power	330PS @ 6200rpm	345PS @ 6200rpm	410PS @ 6700rpm
Torque	300lb ft @ 4500rpm	320lb ft @ 4985rpm	355lb ft @ 5400rpm
Transmission	6-speed manual	6-speed manual	6-speed manual
Brakes	Vented disc/vented disc	Vented disc/vented disc	Vented disc/vented disc
Length/Width/Height	4490/1770/1450mm	4490/1770/1450mm	4490/1770/1450mm
Weight	1400kg	1400kg	1400kg
PERFORMANCE			
Max speed (mph)	157	157	175
0-60mph (secs)	4.5	4.3	3.8
Fuel economy (mpg)	21	20	18
Desirability	★ ★ ★ ★ ★		
Availability	★ ★ ★ ★		
Tuneability	★ ★ ★ ★ ★		

The Evo IX's engine was cleverly tweaked to improve throttle response at low engine speeds.

The Mitsubishi Evo IX was the most cautious and subtlest evolution.

speed and load. MIVEC improved the engine's breathing at high revs to make it more efficient and economical. That in turn meant that Mitsubishi could fit a catalyst with less back pressure, resulting in improved throttle response at low engine speeds.

Low-down torque was also boosted by a longer turbo diffuser. Based on the WRC design, the lengthened housing outlet achieved a 10% improvement in the engine's response throughout the rev range.

In Japan, there remained RS and GSR versions, the former with a five-speed gearbox. In the UK, Mitsubishi launched three Evo IX variants. The FQ-300 was the entry level, with 305PS, 0-62mph in 4.7 secs and, said Mitsubishi, the ability to lap the Nürburgring several seconds faster than the old FQ-300. The midrange FQ-320 boasted tweaks from Ralliart and HKS (a new induction pipe, revised intercooler piping and exhaust), resulting in 326PS and 0-62mph in 4.5 secs. The final FQ-340 got an extra ECU to control ignition timing and air/fuel mixture. Result? 345PS and 0-62mph in 4.3 secs.

Under the skin, very little changed over the VIII MR, which had received a comprehensive Bilstein overhaul. The only suspension change was shorter rear springs, lowering the body and extending rear-end grip. The 4x4 system and transmission were left untouched. The Evolution IX rode on newly developed, lighter Enkei 17 x 8 alloys and 235/45 ZR17 tyres.

Mitsubishi made some effort to make it look different – and more aerodynamic. The redesigned WRC-style grille was integrated into the front bumper and fed more air to the radiator. Circular intakes in the front air dam supplied air to the intercooler pipes. The MR's aluminium roof was carried over on to the IX but a further weight-saving measure was a hollow carbon-fibre rear wing.

The engine's tone now seemed a little more gruff and purposeful. There was less turbo lag and the pull from low revs was much improved, spooling up happily from as low as 2000rpm. The lower-set back end hulked the Evo IX even closer to the tarmac, with less initial understeer.

More Evo extremes

There continued to be a GSR and RS version of each new Evo, as well as an RSII mid-way house. The RS Sprint offered more power (318bhp) and torque (327lb ft) thanks to increased boost and improved induction. The Evo VII Extreme built by Xtreme Autos was a GSR with forged pistons and conrods, high-pressure fuel pump and a more powerful intercooler (339bhp). The Extreme S went even further, being based on the lightweight RS and, with 357bhp, was capable of 0-100mph in under 10 seconds. Top of the pile was the Extreme SC 458 intended for competition and track days, with its 458bhp power output (or over 500bhp if required!). The Evo VIII and IX also evolved into Extreme variations, always backed by a three-year warranty.

A hollow carbon-fibre rear wing was a new weight-saving measure.

SPECIFICATION	Evo IX FQ-300	Evo IX FQ-320	Evo IX FQ-340
Engine	1997cc 4-cyl	1997cc 4-cyl	1997cc 4-cyl
Max power	305PS @ 6950rpm	326PS @ 6700rpm	345PS @ 6800rpm
Torque	297lb ft (403Nm) @ 4400rpm	305lb ft (415Nm) @ 4300rpm	321lb ft (435Nm) @ 4600rpm
Transmission	6-speed manual (RS in Japan: 5-speed manual)		
Brakes	Vented disc/vented disc	Vented disc/vented disc	Vented disc/vented disc
Length/Width/Height	4490/1770/1450mm	4490/1770/1450mm	4490/1770/1450mm
Weight	1400kg	1400kg	1400kg
PERFORMANCE			
Max speed (mph)	157	157	157
0-60mph (secs)	4.7	4.5	4.3
Fuel economy (mpg)	21	21	21
Desirability	★ ★ ★ ★ ★		
Availability	★ ★ ★ ★		
Tuneability	★ ★ ★ ★ ★		

MITSUBISHI GALANT
VR-4 1987-1996

Understated looks for the Galant VR-4 (seen here in 1994).

Not many people know about the Galant VR-4 but this big turbo 4x4 has carved a reputation among enthusiasts for its pace, agility and space – and it donated much of its spec to the legendary Lancer Evolution.

The very first Galant VR-4, launched in 1987, won the Japanese Car of the Year award. Its "Active Four" system referred to the car's four-wheel drive, four-wheel steer, four valves per cylinder, four-wheel anti-lock brakes and four-wheel independent suspension.

Grip was huge from the permanent 4x4 system, while four-wheel steering provided crisp turn-in and manoeuvrability. Optional Electronically Controlled Suspension was the world's first commercial active ride system, limiting body roll.

This was a quick car, too, thanks to its charge-cooled turbocharged 2.0-litre four-cylinder engine. In the first versions, the power output was 205PS, with later examples going up to 220PS. There was also an Eterna ZR-4 model with a five-door hatch body plus a Ralliart-prepared RS model (plus an AMG-badged Galant that was not a VR-4).

The VR-4 continued into a new generation in 1992 but significantly abandoned the Evo-type four-cylinder engine for a 240PS 2.0-litre V6. It continued to look sober (to the point of boring) with a very modest rear spoiler and rather unbecoming alloy wheels. These early generation VR-4s are a rare sight outside Japan but can represent value for money – although running costs are likely to be high.

SPECIFICATION

	1987-91	1992-96
Engine	1997cc 4-cyl	1998cc V6
Max power	205PS (later 220PS) @ 6000 rpm	240PS @ 6000rpm
Torque	217lb ft (294Nm) @ 3000 rpm	228lb ft (309Nm) @ 3500rpm
Transmission	5-speed manual or 4-speed automatic	
Brakes	Vented disc/solid disc	Vented disc/solid disc
Length/Width/Height	4560/1695/1440mm	4630/1730/1410mm
Weight	1370kg	1430kg

PERFORMANCE

Max speed (mph)	135	146
0-60mph (secs)	6.4	6.3
Fuel economy (mpg)	25	22
Desirability	★ ★	
Availability	★	
Tuneability	★ ★ ★	

MITSUBISHI GALANT/LEGNUM
VR-4 1996-2002

Japanese performance cars come in all shapes and sizes. Mitsubishi's Galant VR-4 looks portly and extremely sober but don't be fooled: few cars are as practical, quick or understated as this.

There was a little bit of the Lancer Evo in the VR-4. It had a similar, very sophisticated, permanent four-wheel drive system with a central diff and viscous coupling that split torque between the front and rear axles 50/50. And it came with the same active yaw control system as the Evo V. Unusually for such a high performance machine, you could choose between five-speed manual or five-speed automatic transmission, the latter an

The 1996-2002 Galant VR-4 boasted a twin-turbo engine and four-wheel drive.

The twin-turbo V6 produces 280PS.

The luxurious interior of the VR-4 disguises its sporting pretensions.

INVECS-II Tiptronic-style gearbox (in which case power dropped to 260PS). Equipment was generous – standard air conditioning, power windows, multiple airbags, ABS and Evo-type Active Yaw Control.

The engine was a 2.5-litre 24-valve V6, boosted by twin intercooled turbos to deal up a maximum output of 280PS, as well as plenty of torque. With such a bulky body, roll was more pronounced than the Evo but the VR-4 always felt composed, at the expense of very stiff suspension. This was also a very thirsty car.

The VR-4 came in two specifications, Type S and Type V. The V was slightly lighter, had less sporty wheels and came with more luxury equipment. The S was the "real" VR-4, with wide alloys and a more focused specification. There was also a choice of a four-door saloon or a hugely capacious but heavy estate, badged Legnum, boasting up to 1400 litres of load volume. Perhaps 200 were sold in the UK by Ralliart from 1999 but many more were independently imported. Oil needs changing every 4500 miles and timing belts every 54,000 miles, while gearbox problems can be very costly.

In estate form (badged Legnum in Japan) the VR-4 was an extraordinarily fast load-lugger.

SPECIFICATION	
Engine	2498cc V6
Max power	280PS @ 5500rpm
Torque	267lb ft (363Nm) @ 4000rpm
Transmission	5-speed manual or 5-speed auto
Brakes	Vented disc/solid disc
Length/Width/Height	4630/1740/1420mm
	(Legnum 4680/1740/1450mm)
Weight	1460kg (Legnum 1550kg)
PERFORMANCE	
Max speed (mph)	152
0-60mph (secs)	5.9
Fuel economy (mpg)	18
Desirability	✱ ✱ ✱
Availability	✱ ✱ ✱
Tuneability	✱ ✱ ✱

MITSUBISHI PAJERO
EVOLUTION 1997-1999

Mitsubishi's Pajero Evolution was virtually a Paris-Dakar rally car for the road.

SPECIFICATION
Engine	3497cc V6
Max power	280PS @ 6500rpm
Torque	256lb ft (347Nm) @ 3500rpm
Transmission	5-speed semi-automatic
Brakes	Disc/disc
Length/Width/Height	4075/1875/1915mm
Weight	1985kg

PERFORMANCE
Max speed (mph)	125
0-60mph (secs)	8.0
Fuel economy (mpg)	19
Desirability	★ ★
Availability	★
Tuneability	★ ★

The Pajero has a strong reputation as one of the world's best 4x4 vehicles, but it's usually powered by an unromantic diesel engine. Not so the Pajero Evolution – this had a 280PS MIVEC V6 and enough grunt to overcome the worst terrain at a terrific pace – just like the car that inspired it, Mitsubishi's Paris-Dakar desert racer, which scored 1-2-3 victories two years in a row. It looked a beast with its fat desert racer wings, bonnet bulge, roof fins, angular front bumper with its big air intake, four driving lamps, 9.6-inch ground clearance and drilled sump guard. Inside there was a smattering of carbon-fibre lookalike trim and the larger-than-average hood bulge in your line of sight.

The 4x4 system had Easy Select, allowing you to switch from two to four-wheel drive or vice versa at speeds up to 60mph. There are high and low range four-wheel drive modes, the latter effectively doubling the amount of torque available for very steep gradients. Viscous coupled central differential was standard, as was FTO-derived INVECS Tiptronic-style gearchange, while a hybrid-type limited slip differential was available.

Flooring the throttle produced an almighty lurch forward, the sort of thing that would embarrass most sports cars. However you wouldn't want to argue with a sports car around bends. Despite taut springing, the wallow was enough to wipe the edge off your confidence. It was not the most comfortable riding car in the world either but for sheer road presence, not much can beat the Evolution.

MITSUBISHI
Other models

The AirTrek Turbo R had a 240PS version of the Evo's 4G63 turbo engine.

The RVR Sports Gear was as close to an Evo MPV as any manufacturer has come.

It's too much to call the amazing **Minica Dangan ZZ** a micro-Evo but Mitsubishi can be credited with the honour of inventing a new, and rather bizarre, niche – the performance microcar. The Dangan ZZ was a triumph of technology over dimensions. Its tiny 657cc three-cylinder engine got a turbocharger, fuel injection and no less than five valves per cylinder and a power output of 64PS. It tore up the road, sprinting to 60mph from rest in about 9 seconds and going on to a top speed of 93mph – and that would have been higher if the mandatory speed limiter was removed.

Mitsubishi made a sort of Evo MPV with the **RVR Sports Gear**. For example, the RVR X3 had an Evo 4G63 engine tuned down to 250PS and permanent four-wheel drive. However, despite its extraordinary pace, grip and lairy spoilers, it was no sports car – it weighed 1550kg and had a rather lofty ride height. Ralliart dabbled with importing the RVR into the UK but demand was virtually non-existent.

The **AirTrek Turbo-R** was another sports/SUV crossover vehicle that actually looked quite attractive. Powered by a 240PS version of the 4G63 Evo engine, it featured four-wheel drive and an INVECS II tiptronic gearbox. In other respects it was definitely more SUV than Evo, with, for instance, drum rear brakes and a portly 1520kg kerb weight. It was imported to the UK for £22,995 by Xtreme (ex-Ralliart) but it was always a rare sight.

Australia got its own performance icon with the 2002 **Ralliart Magna**. This big, wild saloon was created by Ralliart Australia. Its 3.5-litre V6 received special pistons, camshafts and ECU for peak power of 241PS at 5500rpm – all transmitted via the front wheels. The Ralliart Magna got a wild-looking body kit featuring a Lancer Evo double-plane rear wing but it remained an Oz-only machine.

The awkwardly-named Dangan ZZ boasted 64bhp and four-wheel drive.

NISSAN
SUNNY
GTI 1992-1994

The 1992 Nissan Sunny GTI boasted 143PS but always looked pale alongside the GTI-R.

SPECIFICATION
Engine	1998cc 4-cyl
Max power	143PS @ 6400rpm
Torque	131lb ft (178Nm) @ 4800rpm
Transmission	5-speed manual (also 4-speed auto)
Brakes	Vented disc/solid disc
Length/Width/Height	3975/1690/1395mm
Weight	1105kg

PERFORMANCE
Max speed (mph)	130
0-60mph (secs)	7.5
Fuel economy (mpg)	34
Desirability	★★
Availability	★★★
Tuneability	★★★★

Nissan first tried a GTI-type Sunny with the dreadful Sunny ZX coupe, sold between 1987 and 1991 – an unpleasant concoction of tacked-on spoilers and a bone-hard ride, alleviated only by decent performance from the 130PS engine.

Far more appealing was the new generation Sunny GTI of 1992. It failed to capitalise on the GTI-R's rally car appearance though: instead Nissan adopted a look so understated that no-one would bat an eyelid as you arrived to buy peas at the local supermarket.

Under the bonnet sat an SR20DE 2.0-litre engine that matched most rivals' power outputs at 143PS. That was enough for a 0-60 time of 7.5 seconds and a top speed of 130mph. It had a broad power band and throttle response was extremely keen, second only to Honda's VTEC.

There was a traction issue in wet conditions, when torque steer took over, but by and large the GTI was a tidy handler. The gearchange quality and brakes were also widely praised.

Often overlooked by enthusiasts, the GTI suffered by association with the ultra-dowdy Sunny it was based on, but it was reliable, quick and easily tuned.

NISSAN SUNNY/PULSAR
GTI-R 1990-1994

When it comes to Japanese four-wheel drive turbocharged rally escapees, the Subaru Impreza and Mitsubishi Evo have been left to clean up. But it could all have been so different. If Nissan had not retired from international rallying, the name GTI-R would be on everyone's lips, for it beat both Subaru and Mitsubishi to the start line by years. The Pulsar GTI-R 4x4 turbo wowed everyone who drove it.

Just look at the statistics. The 2.0-litre turbocharged engine pumped out 220PS, equating to 110PS per litre – more powerful than the original Impreza Turbo and with a better power-to-weight ratio too.

Launched in Japan in August 1990, the Pulsar GTI-R was built to homologate the short-lived Group A rally car. Based on the three-door Pulsar bodyshell, the GTI-R could have passed for a supermarket potterer: the only visible clues to its performance soul were a deeper front spoiler, extrovert rear splitter spoiler and bonnet vents. A prominent bulge with four straked vents cleared the turbo intercooler (mounted on top of the engine), while smaller vents either side provided points for the heated air to exit through.

In Japan only, Nissan also offered a stripped-out lightweight version intended for competition, with 30kg shaved off its weight. In the UK, Nissan imported a mere 70 cars (badged Sunny GTI-R) between April 1992 and February 1993, while the Pulsar GTI-R survived in Japan until December 1994.

The engine was based on the Sunny GTi's 2.0-litre all-aluminium twin cam engine fitted with ECCS multipoint injection and mapping, oil cooler and air-to-air intercooled Garrett T3 turbocharger. If there was one problem, it was the siting of the intercooler – on top of the engine, leading some to nickname it wryly an "interwarmer."

ATTESA four-wheel drive incorporated a viscous centre coupling to create a 50/50 torque split, plus centre and rear limited slip differentials. Suspension was independent by MacPherson struts all round and power steering was standard. The 14-inch seven-spoke alloy wheels looked pretty pokey and many owners upgraded to larger alloys.

To drive, it was effortlessly potent and gloriously accessible. The engine pulled strongly from as low as 2000rpm and tore right up to 7500rpm, on the way displaying very little lag and plenty of torque – all helped by very close-stacked gear ratios. Grip was strong but it was the handling delicacy and balance that really impressed. The brakes were not the GTI-R's strongest suit, though, and it was a noisy car with a stiff ride.

Most GTI-Rs have been substantially modified by now. Check for a smoky engine, although it's pretty noisy and rattly anyway. You may need to reprogramme the ECU for UK fuel if it's an import. Wheel bearings wear, so listen for rumbling sounds. Any whine from the back end means the rear differential is probably on the way out. Any diff is expensive to fix, as are gearbox rebuilds. Check for signs of accident damage and rust on non-undersealed Japanese imports.

It may not have looked much but the GTI-R trailblazed the 4x4 turbo giant-killer idea.

NISSAN SUNNY/PULSAR GTI-R 1990-1994

SPECIFICATION

Engine	1998cc 4-cyl turbo
Max power	220PS @ 6400rpm
Torque	197lb ft @ 4800rpm
Transmission	5-speed manual
Brakes	Vented disc/solid disc
Length/Width/Height	3975/1690/1400mm
Weight	1220kg (lightweight 1190kg)

PERFORMANCE

Max speed (mph)	134 (lightweight 139mph)
0-60mph (secs)	6.1 (lightweight 5.9 secs)
Fuel economy (mpg)	26
Desirability	* * * *
Availability	* *
Tuneability	* * * * *

NISSAN ALMERA
GTI 1996-2000

The Almera GTi (1998 model pictured) looked dowdy but was fun to drive.

If the 1992 Sunny had seemed boring and predictable, the Almera that replaced it made you want to bury your head in the sand, it was so dull.

That was a shame because the GTI version was actually great fun to drive. It shared the same 143PS 2.0-litre twin-cam engine as the old Sunny GTI, so it had decent performance. But the handling was what you bought the GTI for. Quick steering, predictable manners, stiff springing and mild understeer added up to an enthusiast's package, although wet weather grip was a problem.

There was an optional body kit but it did little to improve the Almera's fall-asleep looks. Air conditioning became standard in 1997, while ABS and dual airbags were added from 1999. Nissan knew it was flogging a dead horse and the GTI disappeared from European markets in 2000. The USA got a variant (the Sentra) with a 2.5-litre 175PS engine.

SPECIFICATION	
Engine	1998cc 4-cyl
Max power	143PS @ 6400rpm
Torque	131lb ft (178Nm) @ 4800rpm
Transmission	5-speed manual (also 4-speed auto)
Brakes	Vented disc/solid disc
Length/Width/Height	3975/1690/1395mm
Weight	1105kg
PERFORMANCE	
Max speed (mph)	130
0-60mph (secs)	8.0
Fuel economy (mpg)	34
Desirability	✱ ✱
Availability	✱ ✱ ✱
Tuneability	✱ ✱ ✱ ✱

NISSAN SILVIA
ZX 1983-1988

Silvia has been a tag used on sporting Nissans for quite a while. This handsome coupe is a 1966 Silvia.

Turbocharging arrived with a bang in the Silvia Turbo ZX in 1984.

Nissan invented the Silvia badge as far back as 1965, and it made a name for itself as an adventurously – and sometimes bizarrely – styled mid-size coupé.

In 1983 the latest Silvia arrived, for the first time with the option of a turbocharged engine. Enthusiasts now began to pay attention, especially as this was also the first Silvia to be sold in Europe – thankfully the one with the 1.8-litre CA18 ET turbo engine, developing 135PS.

It was badged Nissan Silvia Turbo ZX and was a true vanguard of turbocharged Japanese performance cars. By today's standards its performance was pretty lukewarm – only 8.9 seconds 0-60 – but its rear-drive handling was certainly entertaining.

A 2.0-litre non-turbo twin-cam ZX was also briefly marketed in some European countries (1984-86), boasting 144PS. Only a three-door hatch was sold in Europe but there was a two-door notchback coupé in some markets, while in the USA there was a 3.0-litre V6 model with 167PS.

SPECIFICATION

	Turbo ZX	ZX
Engine	1809cc 4-cyl	1990cc 4-cyl
Max power	135PS @ 6000rpm	144PS @ 6000rpm
Torque	138lb ft (187Nm) @ 4000rpm	134lb ft (181Nm) @ 4800rpm
Transmission	5-speed manual or 4-speed auto	5-speed manual
Brakes	Vented disc/solid disc	Vented disc/solid disc
Length/Width/Height	4350/1660/1330mm	4350/1660/1330mm
Weight	1136kg	1195kg

PERFORMANCE

	Turbo ZX	ZX
Max speed (mph)	127	129
0-60mph (secs)	8.9	9.0
Fuel economy (mpg)	26	26
Desirability	**	**
Availability	**	**
Tuneability	**	**

NISSAN
SILVIA
S13 180SX/200SX 1988-1994

The Nissan Silvia S13 was known as the 180SX and 200SX in export markets.

The S13 incarnation of the Silvia/SX has become something of a legend, with its delicate rear-drive handling, light weight and decent pace. European markets knew this car as the 200SX. Launched in 1988 in Japan and Europe the year after, it got an uprated 171PS version of the 1.8-litre turbo engine from the previous Silvia, with the intercooler mounted sideways in the front wing.

As for the way it looked, European enthusiasts could be forgiven for thinking that there was only one shape, a three-door 2+2 hatchback with pop-up headlamps. In fact there were many more. In Japan, the Silvia was actually a notchback coupé with a different, fixed-headlamp front end (the hatchback was marketed in Japan as the 180SX). In some markets, a convertible model was also sold. Confusingly, there were also other variations: the convertible came with fixed headlamps or pop-ups and Nissan was even rumoured to have made hatchbacks with fixed lamp front ends (and notchbacks with pop-ups). Why? Because the 180SX was a favourite of the drifting fraternity – that is, street racers who drifted the rear end in lairy oversteering manoeuvres – and when they crashed the car, the fixed-lamp front end was cheaper to replace!

In Japan in 1991, the Silvia range was reorganised around three badges: K's (King), Q's (Queen) and J's (Jack). The Q's got a new 2.0-litre non-turbo 140PS engine, while the K's had a 2.0 Turbo SR20DET engine with 205PS and impressive pace. Let's not forget the American market, which had to make do with the 240SX, a non-turbo 2.4-litre version with 157PS. As a used buy, the SX has an exceptional value-for-talent ratio. It had rather soft suspension from the factory, which only gets softer with passing miles. Still, the handling was always superb and the S13 is in big demand among Japanese performance enthusiasts for its drifting ability, easy tuneability and bargain prices.

SPECIFICATION

	180SX/200SX 1.8	Silvia/180SX 2.0 (Japan only)
Engine	1809cc 4-cyl	1998cc 4-cyl
Max power	171PS @ 6400rpm	205PS @ 6000rpm
Torque	168lb ft (228Nm) @ 4000rpm	202lb ft (275Nm) @ 4000rpm
Transmission	5-sp man or 4-sp auto	5-sp man or 4-sp auto
Brakes	Vented disc/solid disc	Vented disc/solid disc
Length/Width/Height	4470/1690/1290mm	4470/1690/1290mm
Weight	1190kg	1190kg

PERFORMANCE

	180SX/200SX 1.8	Silvia/180SX 2.0 (Japan only)
Max speed (mph)	137	143
0-60mph (secs)	6.9	6.6
Fuel economy (mpg)	26	25
Desirability	★★	★
Availability	★★	
Tuneability	★★★	★★

NISSAN
SILVIA
S14 200SX 1993-2001

Nissan launched the sixth-generation S14 Silvia in Japan in October 1993. This was a physically larger car, now only sold in a single body style – a notchback coupé. Frankly it looked pretty dull and this probably explains why sales never really took off – which does not reflect the car's genuine talent.

Domestically, there was a choice of a normally-aspirated 160PS 2.0-litre engine or a turbo unit with 220PS. When the model arrived in Europe, it was only sold with the turbo engine (though with 200PS) and was called the 200SX.

Like the S13 before it, the S14 Silvia was a much-underrated handling jewel, with crisp, assured rear-drive handling (although it could be a bit of a handful in the wet). Controls were ultra-light, making this as easy as a Micra to tool around town in, and many owners (who tended to be more mature) opted for automatic transmission instead of manual.

In terms of performance, the SR20DET engine did not suffer the same sort of turbo lag as many rivals, enabling the 200SX to record a pretty impressive 0-60 time of just 6.4 seconds. Overtaking was never problematic because of the huge reserves of mid-range power.

In the UK, a Touring pack added a CD, passenger airbag, leather and body kit. There was a facelift in 1996 featuring more aggressive-looking headlamps, new grille, front spoiler and side skirts, but this remained a pretty uninspiring car to look at. Only the Touring version was available after October 1998 in the UK and, although the Silvia was replaced in Japan by the S15 in 1999, the 200SX remained on sale in the UK as late as 2001.

Build quality is superb and reliability one of the best – as long as the car has been serviced properly. Frequent oil changes are recommended (service intervals are every 9000 miles). Panels are easily dented and the paintwork prone to chipping, while expect to suffer turbo and head gasket problems on high-mileage cars.

The US-market S14 was the 240SX which used a 2.4-litre naturally-aspirated engine.

SPECIFICATION	
Engine	1998cc 4-cyl
Max power	200PS @ 6400rpm (Japan 220PS @ 6000rpm)
Torque	195lb ft (265Nm) @ 4000rpm (Japan 275Nm @ 4800rpm)
Transmission	5-speed manual or 4-speed automatic
Brakes	Vented disc/solid disc
Length/Width/Height	4500/1730/1295mm
Weight	1270kg
PERFORMANCE	
Max speed (mph)	146
0-60mph (secs)	6.4
Fuel economy (mpg)	28
Desirability	★ ★ ★
Availability	★ ★ ★
Tuneability	★ ★ ★ ★ ★

The 200SX Touring boasted a leather interior. Space in the back is not over-generous.

NISSAN SILVIA
S15 1999-2002

Lightning bolt on the bonnet for the 1999 Silvia S15.

Spec R models gave 250PS. This one wears the Aero bodykit complete with large rear wing.

A bold lightning strike badge on the bonnet announced the January 1999 arrival of a rather more exciting replacement for the old Silvia S14 (200SX). The new Silvia S15 certainly looked a lot more charismatic and, with its high quality matt plastic, Alfa-style circular air vents, chrome-edged dials and quirky A-pillar mounted boost gauge, it felt better inside too.

Under the skin, its platform was a modest development of the S14's, which meant MacPherson struts up front and multilink suspension at the rear. It also meant that the traditional ultra-sharp turn-in, firm suspension, direct steering and adjustable handling remained.

There were two basic models to choose from, both with developments of the 2.0-litre SR20 engine. The entry-level model was the Spec S, with no turbo, a respectable 165PS and a choice of five-speed manual or four-speed automatic transmission.

By far the more attractive choice was the 250PS turbocharged Spec R, which boasted 30PS more than the old Silvia. A further advantage was a standard six-speed manual gearbox (five speeds in some markets), though you could opt for a four-speed automatic transmission if you could put up with 25PS less power.

An option for both Spec R and Spec S models was an "Aero" bodykit, featuring an enormous rear aerofoil. In July 2000, Autech (a Nissan subsidiary) launched a convertible version called the Varietta, with Japan's first-ever electric folding metal top; it folded away in only 20 seconds. When the S15 left production in 2002, the Silvia name died with it. At least the badge had gone out on a high note, and the S15 is well appreciated by those who know about it – even though it's grey import only.

SPECIFICATION

	Spec S	Spec R
Engine	1998cc 4-cyl	1998cc 4-cyl
Max power	165PS @ 6400rpm	250PS @ 6400rpm (225PS auto)
Torque	141lb ft (192Nm) @ 4800rpm	202lb ft (275Nm) @ 4800rpm
Transmission	5-speed manual or 4-speed auto	5 or 6-speed manual or 4-speed auto
Brakes	Vented disc/solid disc	Vented disc/solid disc
Length/Width/Height	4445/1695/1285mm	4445/1695/1285mm
Weight	1240kg	1240kg

PERFORMANCE

Max speed (mph)	130	149
0-60mph (secs)	7.8	6.0
Fuel economy (mpg)	31	26
Desirability	***	
Availability	**	
Tuneability	****	

NISSAN
300ZX & FAIRLADY Z

1989-2000

Nissan catapulted itself into the supercar league with the 1990 300ZX Turbo.

If you're an English speaker, "Fairlady" is a frankly ludicrous name for a car. It sounds like a car with pink fur seats, rather than what it has been since 1959: Nissan's most sporty model.

The early Fairladys were hardly known outside Japan but that all changed in 1969, when Nissan launched the first Fairlady Z, mercifully rebadged 240Z in export markets. During the 1970s, it became the world's best-selling sports car, offering graceful looks, decent performance and a bargain price.

In subsequent generations, the Z grew more corpulent and decidedly less and less like a sports car. The 300ZX series of 1983-1989 was particularly blancmange-like to drive. That trend changed dramatically in February 1989, when the all-new Z32-series 300ZX was launched at the Chicago Motor Show.

This ZX was a very different animal – something approaching a genuine supercar. Like many Japanese cars of the time, it was a technological tour de force. The new coupé had a 3.0-litre V6 engine (with twin turbos in most markets), variable valve timing and multilink rear suspension with HICAS active four-wheel steering.

It looked the part too and was clearly gunning for Porsche. In terms of handling at least, it succeeded. Despite its generous dimensions, the 300ZX was spectacularly well balanced and a lot of fun – certainly one of the most entertaining chassis ever to come out of Japan. Yet it was so easy to drive, both in town and on long motorway cruises.

The version imported into Europe was the 2+2 Twin Turbo. Officially rated at 283PS, this engine was a firecracker, boasting excellent torque and superb performance (155mph top speed, 0-60 in 5.6 seconds). It got rave reviews, was practical with its three-door coupé layout and was well-equipped, but it was pretty expensive and always suffered in terms of image because it was sold alongside Micras. The 300ZX was withdrawn from sale in the UK at the end of 1994, partly because of problems meeting EU emissions requirements but also because sales had reduced to a mere trickle. However, production continued for Japan until 2000.

In Japan there were several Z versions never seen elsewhere. For starters, there was a more overtly sporting short-wheelbase two-seater. It was some 185mm shorter in the wheelbase, weighed substantially less and traded rear seat space (token in the 2+2) for extra boot volume, and was widely regarded as having the more agile chassis.

Many Zs were fitted with a T-Top targa roof consisting of two glass lift-out roof panels. Another model that the USA and Japan also received from 1992 (but never officially in Europe) was the convertible, an

Japanese-only 300ZX Version R gained a stiffer body and uprated brakes.

In Japan the 300ZX was badged Fairlady Z – this is a 1998 example.

NISSAN 300ZX & FAIRLADY Z 1989-2000

A convertible two-seater was marketed in the USA and Japan from 1992.

extremely smart full open-roof two-seater. It's much rarer to find but it is certainly exclusive.

In Japan there was also a normally-aspirated model with 230PS, which was cheaper to buy and run but never had the same scorching appeal as the Twin Turbo model.

To summarise Japanese development, a Series 2 model arrived in 1992, boasting a hydraulic HICAS system and driver airbag. The Series 3 a year later added a taller rear spoiler, remote locking and electronic HICAS 2. The Series 4 of 1994-1997 was available in luxury Version S guise, the Series 5 of 1997 in Version R guise (stiffer body, better brakes) and the run-out Series 6 of 1998-2000 had revised front and rear spoilers, HID headlamps and white dials.

A 300ZX can make a great buy. It has huge talent but is regarded as somehow down-market and uncouth. Used prices tend to be rock-bottom. Manual gearboxes can suffer with heavy use, which is why many people actually prefer the automatic. The engine is pretty reliable but the twin turbos can cause problems, especially if there are gaps in maintenance – look carefully for smoke. The V6 engine is eminently tuneable and many cars have substantial power upgrades – check what's been done and who's done it. Exhausts are very expensive to replace, while the rear-steer HICAS system comes in silicon-filled bushes – if worn, the whole assembly needs to be (expensively) replaced. T-Tops are prone to leaks but otherwise the bodywork should be perfect.

SPECIFICATION		
	Twin-Turbo	Non-Turbo
Engine	2960cc V6	2960cc V6
Max power	283PS @ 6400rpm (auto 268PS)	230PS @ 6400rpm
Torque	286lb ft (388Nm) @ 3600rpm (auto 272lb ft (370Nm) @ 3200rpm)	201lb ft (273Nm) @ 4800rpm
Transmission	5-speed manual or 4-speed auto	5-speed manual or 4-speed auto
Brakes	Vented disc/vented disc	Vented disc/vented disc
Length/Width/Height	4520/1790/1250 (2-seater 4305mm long)	
Weight	1510kg	1450kg (cabrio 1480kg)
PERFORMANCE		
Max speed (mph)	155	146
0-60mph (secs)	5.6	6.8
Fuel economy (mpg)	18	20
Desirability	★ ★ ★	
Availability	★ ★ ★ ★	
Tuneability	★ ★ ★ ★	

NISSAN 350Z

2002-date

Few sports car launches of the last 20 years have been so ecstatically greeted as the Nissan 350Z's. Here was a car with European engineering standards, Japanese quality, and brilliant styling from Nissan's American studio. When Nissan launched the 350Z in 2002 (Europe in 2003), it had one crucial ingredient lacking in many contemporary Japanese coupés: desirability.

Nissan played heavily on the 350Z's heritage, recalling the glory days of the 240Z. Not only did the 350Z look fabulous, it was a great place to sit. You sat very low down – great for seat-of-the-pants feel – and your view included an evocative exposed rear strut brace. Cowled instruments recalled the 240Z while an optional GT Pack included heated leather seats, Bose sound system and cruise control.

The glorious 3.5-litre V6 (actually an eight-year old unit by 2002) sounded amazing and delivered a class-leading 280PS without turbocharging. Power was transmitted to the rear wheels via a lightweight one-piece carbon fibre propeller shaft and close-ratio six-speed gearbox (a Tiptronic-style automatic was available in Japan but not Europe).

As for handling, Nissan's sophisticated suspension set-up and rear-wheel drive paid dividends. There was multi-link independent suspension all round, using forged aluminium components in subframes, plus big 18-inch alloy wheels. The chassis was extremely grippy, even in wet conditions thanks to an effective traction control system, while its balance impressed all who drove it. With superbly-weighted steering that let you know exactly what was happening up at the front

Engaging interior design for the two-seater 350Z.

With the 2002 350Z, Nissan scored a knockout hit.

NISSAN 350Z 2002-DATE

Roadster version managed to keep its body rigidity intact.

SPECIFICATION		
	350Z	**350Z 35th Anniversary**
Engine	3498cc V6	3498cc V6
Max power	280PS @ 6200rpm	300PS @ 6400rpm
Torque	267lb ft (363Nm) @ 4800rpm	260lb ft (353Nm) @ 4800rpm
Transmission	6-sp man (also 5-sp auto in Japan)	6-sp man
Brakes	Vented disc/vented disc	Vented disc/vented disc
Length/Width/Height	4310/1815/1315mm	4310/1815/1315mm
Weight	1525kg (Roadster 1645kg)	1545kg
PERFORMANCE		
Max speed (mph)	155	155
0-60mph (secs)	5.9 (Roadster 6.4 secs)	5.8
Fuel economy (mpg)	25	25
Desirability	* * * * *	
Availability	* * * *	
Tuneability	* * * * *	

end and sharp Brembo brakes, this was a brilliant driver's car.

A convertible Roadster version arrived in 2004 in the USA and Japan, finally reaching Europe in 2005. This had a strengthened bodyshell to minimise the effects of chopping the roof off; the vinyl top folded electrically in under 20 seconds.

In 2004-2005, Nissan launched a 35th Anniversary edition (initially called GT4 in the UK). They gave the V6 engine revised pistons and camshafts, plus electronic exhaust valve timing control. This helped produce an extra 20PS to reach 300PS at 6400rpm (200rpm higher than the standard car). However torque dropped slightly. Acceleration was slightly improved, as was the exhaust note. The only other major changes were unique 18-inch alloy wheels, a dash plaque and a choice of black or yellow paint.

2003 Nissan 350Z with Nismo bodykit.

A 35th Anniversary special edition was launched to celebrate 35 years since the launch of the original Z-car, the 240Z.

NISSAN SKYLINE

GT-R R32 1989-1994

Skyline is Nissan's oldest nameplate, dating way back to 1955. It always denoted Nissan's high-spec, high-performance range but the iconic GT-R badge was not created until 1969 when Nissan launched its first homologation racer. The Skyline badge muddled on through the 1970s and 1980s but it was not until the eighth-generation Skyline R32 was launched in GT-R guise that Nissan revolutionised all the parameters. The GT-R instantly became a modern supercar icon.

For a start, there was Nissan's ATTESA four-wheel drive system. Speed sensors on all four wheels, together with g-sensors and throttle/brake sensors, analysed the car's traction, as well as every nuance of the driver's input, every 100th of a second. Up to 50% of the engine's torque could then be directed to the front wheels to keep things stable.

HICAS four-wheel steering employed multiple sensors to detect steering input, the rate at which the wheel was being turned, the car's speed and the lateral g-forces at work. It then decided on the amount of rear-wheel steer to apply, up to a maximum of 0.5 degrees. When entering a bend at speed, the rear wheels turned the opposite way to the front wheels to enable fast turn-in. Then the wheels turned the other way to settle the car into a stable attitude, so that understeer was minimised.

The rest of the specification looked pretty mouth-watering, including multilink front and rear suspension and all-round ventilated disc brakes with four-piston front callipers. From 1993 there was also a V-Spec model with four-pot Brembos up front and two-pot Brembos at the rear, retuned four-wheel drive, revised front suspension and larger-diameter 17-inch alloy wheels and tyres.

The RB26 DETT engine was an amazing power-plant: a 2.6-litre straight six with four valves per cylinder, an aluminium twin cam head and twin Garrett ceramic turbochargers. Nissan had to do a lot to keep the power output down to the Japanese maximum of 280PS, with the result that this is one of the most tuneable engines in existence. Putting a new chip in to boost power became almost obligatory and the sky is the limit as far as tuning potential goes. Examples have been known to run as high as 1200bhp! You need to uprate the underpinnings, including clutch, gearbox and brakes, if serious tuning is intended.

A whale-tail rear spoiler, deep front spoiler, flared wings and fat alloy wheels were the only things that

This is where the GT-R legend began: the 1969 Nissan Skyline GT-R. The GT-R bloodline flowered in the 1990s into the supercar nicknamed "Godzilla".

SPECIFICATION	
Engine	2568cc 6-cyl
Max power	280PS @ 6800rpm
Torque	260lb ft (353Nm) @ 4400rpm
Transmission	5-speed manual
Brakes	Vented disc/vented disc
Length/Width/Height	4545/1755/1340mm
Weight	1430kg
PERFORMANCE	
Max speed (mph)	155
0-60mph (secs)	5.1
Fuel economy (mpg)	17
Desirability	* * * *
Availability	* * *
Tuneability	* * * * *

NISSAN SKYLINE GT-R R32 1989-1994

made the two-door GT-R stand out. Inside too it all looked very sober, even down-market.

In the GT-R R32, Nissan created one of the quickest, most memorable driving machines in history. By keeping the rev band high enough to maintain maximum turbo boost, you were never off the pace. The steering was quick and full of feel, the huge brakes massively powerful, and even the ride was fairly compliant. It instantly became the stuff of legends.

Some 40,390 standard R32 GT-Rs were sold, plus 1453 V-Spec and 1303 -Spec II versions. Many were imported as "greys" into the UK and there are quite a few to choose from second-hand. The good news is that this is an incredibly strong car. Engines are robust, although turbos are known to blow with age, while engines benefit from frequent oil changes (and the fitment of an oil cooler).

The standard clutch wears quickly while the gearbox can get expensively graunchy. Brembo brakes and pads are costly to replace, as are tyres. Most GT-Rs will have been tuned (often to an extraordinary degree), so you need to be careful and make sure the previous owner did not skimp. Very few original cars remain but a simple chip, bigger exhaust and air filter can transform the performance for very little outlay.

The nickname "Godzilla" stuck for the astonishing Skyline GT-R R32.

NISSAN SKYLINE
GT-R R33 1995-1998

The Skyline R33 was launched in 1994 as a direct replacement for the R32, although the GT-R version did not arrive until January 1995. Despite its bigger, more curvaceous body style, this was very much an evolution of the R32.

Body modifications improved the Cd figure from an unexceptional 0.40 down to 0.35 (despite a larger frontal area than the R32). Also there was a new four-way adjustable rear spoiler to fine-tune downforce. Although the weight went up compared to the R32, the weight distribution was better.

The engine remained very much the same, with twin Garrett turbochargers, twin cams, 24 valves and an output of 280PS. However more torque was liberated thanks to an uprated intercooler, higher peak boost and an enhanced management computer.

Underneath, new two-arm upper front multilink suspension, increased rear suspension travel and stiffer anchor points improved handling. Equally important were some structural changes that boosted overall stiffness, such as strut bars front and rear, an extra panel behind the rear seats and extra cross-bars in the floor.

Another important change was new yaw rate feedback for the Super HICAS four-wheel steer system, plus full electronic control, making the handling even more sure-footed. The R33 gained the R32 V-Spec's Brembo race-spec brakes as standard, with revised ABS control parameters. The wheels grew in size too, to 17x9J five-spokers, shod with 245/45ZR tyres. On the safety side, there was a driver's air bag and, in later cars, a passenger air bag.

Again there was a V-Spec model, with uprated four-wheel drive, active limited slip differential and lower, harder suspension. If you really want something special, you might try a Nismo 400R. It was much more expensive (around twice as much), but you got a bigger RBX-GT2 2.8-litre engine with a 10,000rpm redline and 400PS, Nismo brakes and intercooler, huge 18-inch wheels with 275/35 ZR18 tyres, Bilstein gas dampers, lower suspension, torque split controller and a special Nismo aero body kit and spoiler. Only 99 such cars were built. There was also a very rare four-door GT-R made in 1998 only, plus two limited edition models (1996 LM Limited and 1997 V-Spec N1 stripped-out virtual racer).

Once more, the cockpit reflected the fact that the GT-R was based on a fairly run-of-the-mill model. Its sombre black trim was only alleviated by attractive seats, some carbon-fibre trim and alluring GT-R graphics.

The R33's intelligent split-torque four-wheel drive system, combined with electronic limited slip diff and active rear-wheel steer, gave it even more controllable cornering. This was one of the world's quickest cars on winding roads, as confirmed by Nissan's attainment of the lap record for production cars at the Nürburgring in Germany. No doubt about it, this was one of the world's great driver's cars.

The R33 GT-R left production in December 1998 ahead of a much-improved R34. It was only sold officially in Japan and Australia, although Nissan did sell 100 examples in the UK market in 1997. As so little changed from the R32, you need to look out for exactly the same things when buying used.

The enlarged Skyline GT-R R33 was an even more formidable beast.

NISSAN SKYLINE GT-R R33 1995-1998

SPECIFICATION

	R33	Nismo 400R
Engine	2568cc 6-cyl	2771cc 6-cyl
Max power	280PS @ 6800rpm	400PS @ 6800rpm
Torque	271lb ft (368Nm) @ 4400rpm	352lb ft (478Nm) @ 4400rpm
Transmission	5-speed manual	5-speed manual
Brakes	Vented disc/vented disc	Vented disc/vented disc
Length/Width/Height	4675/1780/1360mm	4675/1830/1330mm
Weight	1530kg	1550kg

PERFORMANCE

Max speed (mph)	155	n/a
0-60mph (secs)	5.1	n/a
Fuel economy (mpg)	17	n/a
Desirability	*****	
Availability	****	
Tuneability	*****	

NISSAN SKYLINE
GT-R R34 1999-2002

With the GT-R R34, Nissan reduced size and boosted performance.

If you're into Skylines, the GT-R R34 is Godzilla. Nothing beats it for pace, presence or tuneability. Launched in January 1999, the R34 evolved to face the critics of the R33, who said that it had become too bulky. The R34 was therefore significantly smaller and was not only more rounded in terms of driving character, but much quicker too.

Despite the fact that it was essentially an evolution of the R33 GT-R, the R34 looked like an all-new car. The front spoiler was even deeper and more brutal, the sides were more chiselled, the wide rear wing line kicked up purposefully with a meaty bulge above the arch, and the dramatic rear spoiler was more aggressive.

The bodyshell became a lot stiffer so the handling showed a marked improvement. There were even carbon-fibre covers under the engine and rear axle to ease airflow over these obtrusive elements. But despite weight-saving measures and its smaller size, the R34 was actually slightly heavier than the R33.

The 2.6-litre straight six engine evolved as well. Off-boost performance was improved by new Garrett ball-bearing ceramic turbochargers and revised cam and valve timing. There was now much less turbo lag (the turbos coming on song below 3000rpm) and less need to hoof the throttle. The power output was almost always a lot higher than the stated 280PS – more like 300-320PS.

The computer brains behind the HICAS four-wheel steering and four-wheel drive system were much faster

NISSAN SKYLINE GT-R R34 1999-2002

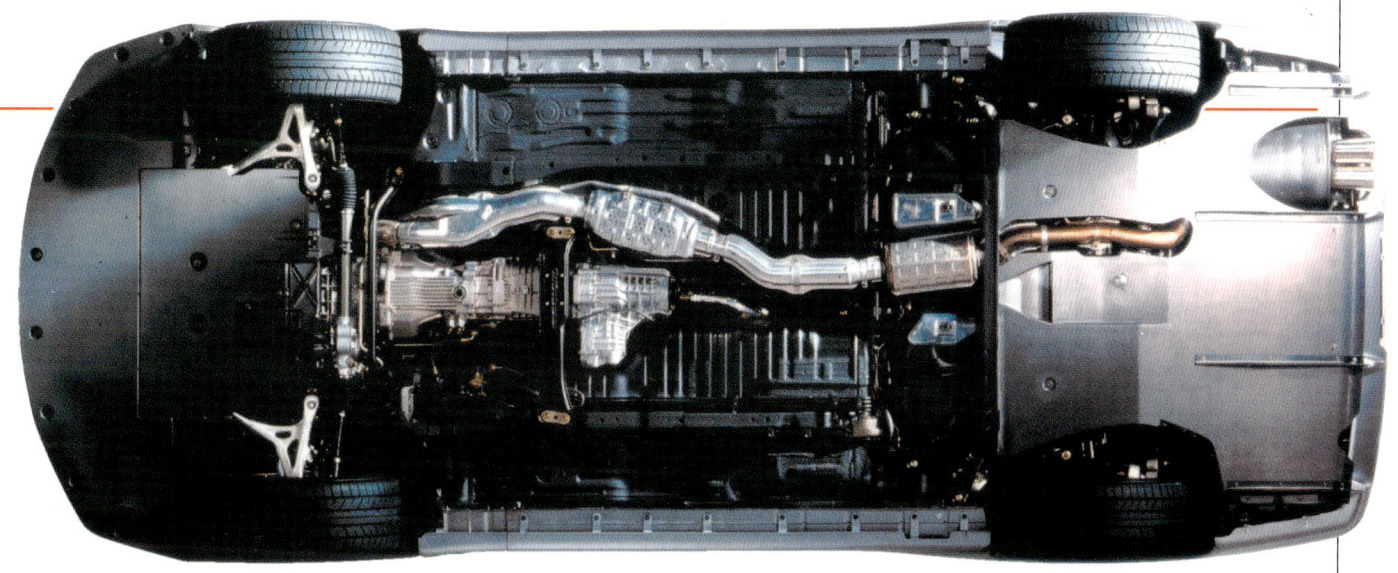

Sophisticated four-wheel drive and smooth undertray helped legendary dynamics.

2002 R34 Nür edition came with no air con and an N1-spec engine

NISSAN SKYLINE GT-R R34 1999-2002

The GT-R R-34 had much more brutal styling than its predecessor.

Useful multi-function screen livened up an otherwise lacklustre cabin.

NISSAN SKYLINE GT-R R34 1999-2002

Uncanny levels of grip and extraordinary tuneability appealed to enthusiastic drivers.

than before. It now took even less time to calculate inputs as diverse as steering angle, throttle opening and yaw rate to deliver the optimum amount of torque to the correct wheel. The R34 also had a much more composed ride and an even more uncanny ability to stay on line through difficult corners. One of the biggest improvements was the gearbox, a Getrag six-speeder with closer ratios than before. The gearchange was better, with less movement and more precision.

Another area of great improvement was the interior. The seats were superbly shaped for extreme cornering, the steering wheel was chunkier and the ergonomics even better. A great selling point was the neat LCD multi-function display atop the dash with its bar graph readings for seven different ancillary functions, from boost pressure to exhaust temperature.

Once again there were standard and V-Spec versions, the latter with ATTESA E-TS PRO four-wheel drive, active rear diff, lower, harder suspension and a g-meter in the multi-function display. There were some interesting special editions: a launch one with Midnight Purple paint, the 2000 V-Spec II with carbon-fibre bonnet and NACA duct, 2001 M-Spec with leather trim and softer dampers, stripped-out N1 racing versions and 2002 Nür editions with no air con and an N1-spec engine. Official UK imports began in 2000, based on the Japanese V-Spec with some modifications, including oil coolers for the engine, gearbox and transfer box, a Nismo ECU, Nismo multi-function display and full leather trim.

As ever, the RB26DETT engine is bomb-proof as long as the oil and filters have been changed regularly and it hasn't been over-revved. The standard exhaust is pretty restrictive, so many examples have been freed up with wide-bore systems. Gearboxes sound noisy at the best of times but are pretty reliable. Watch out for warped or scored brake discs – they cost loads to replace.

SPECIFICATION	
Engine	2568cc 6-cyl
Max power	280PS @ 6800rpm
Torque	289lb ft (392Nm) @ 4400rpm
Transmission	6-speed manual
Brakes	Vented disc/vented disc
Length/Width/Height	4600/1785/1360 mm
Weight	1560kg
PERFORMANCE	
Max speed (mph)	155
0-60mph (secs)	4.5
Fuel economy (mpg)	20
Desirability	★ ★ ★ ★ ★
Availability	★ ★ ★ ★
Tuneability	★ ★ ★ ★ ★

NISSAN
SKYLINE
GT 1989-2002

It looked similar to a GT-R and also had 280PS but the GTS was not quite in the same league.

SPECIFICATION

	R32 GTSt	R33 GTS25t	R34 25GTT
Engine	1998cc 6-cyl	2498cc 6-cyl	2498cc 6-cyl
Max power	215PS @ 6400rpm	250PS @ 6400rpm	280PS @ 6400rpm
Torque	195lb ft (265Nm) @ 3200rpm	217lb ft (295Nm) @ 4800rpm	250lb ft (338Nm) @ 3200rpm
Transmission	5-sp man or 4-sp auto	5-sp man or 4-sp auto	5-sp man or 4-sp auto
Brakes	Vented disc/vented disc	Vented disc/vented disc	Vented disc/vented disc
Length/Width/Height	4530/1695/1325mm	4640/1720/1340mm	4580/1725/1340mm
Weight	1320kg	1360kg	1410kg

PERFORMANCE

	R32 GTSt	R33 GTS25t	R34 25GTT
Max speed (mph)	143	149	155
0-60mph (secs)	7.2	6.7	6.2
Fuel economy (mpg)	26	24	23
Desirability	* * *		
Availability	* *		
Tuneability	* * * * *		

NISSAN SKYLINE GT 1989-2002

While the Skyline GT-R may grab all the headlines and the lust, there has always been a sub-species of Skyline that has gained a big following over the years. It's not a GT-R but it's not far off.

That model is the Skyline GT, first seen in 1989 and offered ever since. It may not have the stratospheric performance or uncanny grip of the GT-R but it has its own set of strengths. The first of those is obviously price. You can buy and run a lesser Skyline for much less than a GT-R.

So what exactly is a GT? It's essentially a less powerful rear-drive, 2.5-litre Skyline. It doesn't have quite the same radical styling – although sometimes you have to look twice to spot the differences. Not only does the body look very similar, it has all the strength of the GT-R shell.

The first model, the R32 GTS, had an RB20DE non-turbo 2.0-litre six-cylinder unit with only 155PS, though a GTS-t turbo version with 215PS was also produced (also available with four-wheel drive). A 2.5-litre six-cylinder RB25DE engined GTS25 arrived in 1991, with 190PS.

The "real thing" arrived in 1993: the R33 GTS25t, sporting a turbo version of the 2.5 engine and a more impressive 250PS. The R34 was also sold as the 25GT Turbo (GTT) with this engine, but now with 280PS.

The GT series was most commonly rear-wheel drive (some four-wheel drive versions were built too). It always came with either a five-speed manual or four-speed automatic gearbox. And its engine was tuned more for torque response than outright power: the linear charge turbocharger ran a lower boost. The power did not really come in until around 4000rpm and it was not the smoothest six ever seen.

There was less mechanical and electrical complexity, while some testers thought the rear-drive handling was even more engaging than the GT-R's. It still kept HICAS rear-wheel steer, incidentally. Performance was strong – the GT weighed a lot less than the GT-R – while there were also four-door GT models as well as two-door coupes.

Like the GT-R, the engine is virtually bomb-proof but better to change the oil every 5000 miles or so. The only major problem seems to be warped exhaust manifolds. Brake discs can be costly to replace, and check for worn suspension bushes, uneven tyre wear and split body welds which can indicate crash damage. Some cars have been converted with body kits to look like GT-Rs but are never entirely convincing.

The turbocharged 2498cc straight-six engine gave 250PS in the R33 GT.

Automatic transmission was a popular option for the GTS (R33 version pictured).

The Skyline GTS was also available as a rather discreet four-dour saloon.

NISSAN
SKYLINE
350 GT 2003-date

The Skyline 350 GT (Infiniti G35 in the US) was a pale follow-up to the GT-R legend.

Huge speculation surrounded what would replace the fabulous Skyline GT-R R34. The answer, it seemed, was nothing – for when the new Skyline appeared in 2001 it was only sold in four-door saloon form, and there was no GT-R.

Some excitement was created in 2003 when Nissan announced a two-door coupé Skyline model, the 350 GT (sold in the USA as the Infiniti G35). However, this was no four-wheel drive turbocharged monster but a longer, taller, four-seat evolution of the 350Z.

The new 350 GT owed most of its spec to the 350Z, including its 280PS V6 engine, transmission and most of its suspension. Weight was only slightly up compared to the 350Z but performance was definitely blunted.

The prospect of a genuine Skyline GT-R was kept alive by Nissan showing a GT-R concept car at various shows from 2001, which featured 350Z-inspired coupé bodywork, but no definite announcement had been made by the time of writing.

SPECIFICATION	
Engine	3498cc V6
Max power	280PS @ 6200rpm
Torque	267lb ft (363Nm) @ 4800rpm
Transmission	6-speed manual or 5-sp auto
Brakes	Vented disc/vented disc
Length/Width/Height	4640/1815/1395mm
Weight	1530kg
PERFORMANCE	
Max speed (mph)	149
0-60mph (secs)	6.5
Fuel economy (mpg)	23
Desirability	* * * *
Availability	* *
Tuneability	* * *

NISSAN
Other Models

The 1989 March Super Turbo produced 110PS from only 903cc.

The Stagea RS – not quite a Skyline GT-R estate, but almost.

Nissan's smallest car in the 1990s was the Micra (March in Japan). There was a hilarious **March Super Turbo** from 1989 which got a turbocharged and supercharged all-aluminium 930cc engine with no less than 110PS. It got an aero body kit but it kept its drum brakes and old-fashioned rear suspension, so it was always a stinker to drive.

The same could be said of the **Sunny 1500 Turbo Nismo**. Despite its lofty badging, this coupé and three-door hatch offered from 1985 was no performance icon. And despite its turbocharger, Nissan's retro **Figaro** – based on the March platform – is less about performance and more about pastiche. This automatic-only canvas-top bijou has become the darling of fashionistas in recent times and we should really hurry on by.

Moving up, Nissan made a high performance estate car that has sometimes been described as a Skyline GT-R estate. That's overstating things, perhaps, but Nissan's **Stagea RS** did boast a 280PS six-cylinder engine and four-wheel drive, as well as an enormous load capacity.

In a book called Japanese Performance Cars, some mention ought to be made of the staggering 1997 **R390 GT1**, even though only one thinly disguised roadgoing Le Mans racer was ever made (for homologation purposes). It was however offered built-to-order for road use at $1 million. Some vital statistics: 200mph top speed, 0-60 in 4.1 seconds, six-speed sequential gearbox. Nismo developed the 3.5-litre twin turbo V8 engine, producing an estimated 350PS in road spec. UK-based TWR developed the suspension along with most of the rest of the car.

The amazing R390 GT1 which was built as a road car to homologate the racer.

135

SUBARU
XT & ALCYONE

1985-1990

Subaru was the absolute pioneer of four-wheel drive in mass-market road cars. But its initial forays in the 1970s were all utilitarian. The first real attempt at a performance machine was the curious Alcyone of 1985. Alcyone was the domestic market name for the model (a bright star in the Pleiades); in the USA and Europe it was simply called the Subaru XT.

Supposedly evoking "the aerodynamic shape of a hawk or eagle," its shape boasted the world's lowest coefficient of drag at 0.29 at the time. But its ultra-straight styling looked gawky and its interior was an exercise in pure gimmickry, featuring an L-shaped steering wheel and Star Trek-style console.

It did have full-time 4x4 transmission, but its floorpan was basically shared with the humble Subaru Leone and it could never be described as a sports car. It was overpriced, anaemic and very little fun to pilot. It wasn't even powerful. The version sold in Europe had a 136PS 1.8 flat-four turbo engine but there were also non-turbo versions in Japan and a 2.7-litre straight-six XT6 version for the USA and Japan with up to 147PS. Worth considering? Only for curiosity value, but frankly the XT is a grade one lemon.

The XT's interior was pretty unconventional.

The XT/Alcyone was Subaru's first ever coupe but it was frankly a bizarre, lame conception.

SPECIFICATION	
Engine	1781cc flat-four
Max power	136PS @ 5600rpm
Torque	145lb ft (196Nm) @ 2800rpm
Transmission	5-speed manual or 4-speed auto
Brakes	Vented disc/solid disc
Length/Width/Height	4450/1692/1293mm
Weight	1145kg
PERFORMANCE	
Max speed (mph)	124
0-60mph (secs)	9.5
Fuel economy (mpg)	29
Desirability	*
Availability	*
Tuneability	* *

SUBARU
SVX & ALCYONE

1991-1996

No car shows Japan's leap from dull to dramatic more than the Subaru SVX, which was an unbelievable jump up from the "Mad Hatter" XT. As a package it was unique, with an extraordinary 3.3-litre flat-six 230PS engine mounted up front, driving all four wheels. Its Giugiaro-styled concept-car looks were utterly individual and you could hardly fail to raise a Roger Moore eyebrow at its windows-within-windows glass treatment. Its arsenal of hi-tech gadgets included variable induction and permanent 4x4 with a centre diff to transfer more torque to the wheels with most grip.

It had a solid handling/ride mix, refined yet poised through bends. Being a bit of a heavyweight and only available with a four-speed automatic, it was not supercar-fast: a 144mph top speed and a 0-60 time of 8.7 seconds were respectable in the grand tourer class in which the SVX competed.

It was only sold in the UK between 1992 and 1996 and is rarer than Colgate for chickens. Because of its obscurity you can pick one up for peanuts.

As for reliability, the SVX is superbly built and very durable. But it's complex and so you need a full service record – ideally from one of Subaru's nominated Advanced Vehicle Centres. The electrics should be checked out, especially the electric seats, heated mirrors and climate control. The bumpers, lower doors, rear quarter panels and bootlid are made of composites and should be checked carefully for cracks and poor paintwork.

The unique naturally-aspirated 3.3-litre flat-six engine produced 230PS.

SPECIFICATION	
Engine	3318cc flat-six
Max power	230PS @ 5600rpm
Torque	228lb ft (309Nm) @ 4800rpm
Transmission	4-speed automatic
Brakes	Vented disc/vented disc
Length/Width/Height	4625/1770/1300mm
Weight	1580kg
PERFORMANCE	
Max speed (mph)	144
0-60mph (secs)	8.7
Fuel economy (mpg)	24
Desirability	* * *
Availability	* *
Tuneability	*

SUBARU IMPREZA
TURBO 1994-2000

Subaru's Impreza Turbo delivered pace, grip and value – none more so than the RB5 pictured.

World Rally conqueror, practical everyday transport, blistering performance road car icon – the Subaru Impreza Turbo had it all. Its four-wheel drive transmission, flat-four turbocharged engine and unpretentious appearance made it unique in the car world, while its astonishing pace and uncanny cornering ability made it an absolute legend among enthusiasts.

The Impreza was launched in Japan in November 1992, including the 240PS turbocharged WRX (see separate entry). Europe had to wait until March 1994 for a detuned version of the WRX, badged Turbo 2000 in the UK. It kept the fabulous 2.0-litre turbocharged flat-four engine format but used a smaller IHI turbocharger which favoured low-end torque and minimal turbo lag. It pumped out less power than the WRX (211PS) but this was still enough for supercar-slaying pace. The five-speed manual transmission had wider-spaced ratios than the WRX and a more long-legged final drive ratio, suiting European driving conditions better – and it still posted faster in-gear times than a Porsche Boxster.

Crucial to the overall dynamics was the all-wheel drive system. Like most 4x4 turbocharged cars, there

was a free differential in the front axle that had no wheelspin limiting mechanism. The centre differential was a viscous coupling device that, in normal circumstances, split the torque 50-50 front-rear. A second viscous coupler was fitted in the rear differential to split torque to each of the rear wheels. This made it supremely safe and predictable even in very slippery conditions. Braking by ventilated front discs and solid rears was exceptional too, helped by standard ABS (in the UK at least).

From launch there were four and five-door Turbo models. On the saloon, the boomerang-shaped rear spoiler sat atop the boot. For the five-door, there were two spoilers, one at roof level and one at waist level. The early Turbo had 15-inch wheels, upgraded in 1998 to 16 inches.

The Impreza was an odd mixture of quirkiness (the five-door version especially) and innocuous styling – despite the Turbo's deep front spoiler, large integral spotlights, bonnet vents and scoops, side skirts and rear spoiler. Inside it was downbeat, too, looking rather sombre and cheap, but it was highly practical and well-equipped.

Road testers found it could leave the Escort

Odd-looking it may have been but the practical five-door wagon was just as fast as the saloon.

SUBARU IMPREZA TURBO 1994-2000

SPECIFICATION

	Turbo 2000	Prodrive PPP
Engine	1994cc flat-four	1994cc flat-four
Max power	211PS @ 6000rpm (218PS @ 5600rpm from 1998)	240PS @ 6000rpm
Torque	201lb ft (270Nm) @ 4800rpm (later 214lb ft (290Nm) @ 4000rpm)	258lb ft (350Nm) @ 3500rpm
Transmission	5-speed manual	5-speed manual
Brakes	Vented disc/solid disc	Vented disc/solid disc
Length/Width/Height	4340/1690/1400mm (estate 1435mm high)	
Weight	1213kg	1235kg

PERFORMANCE

Max speed (mph)	137 (144mph from 1998)	145
0-60mph (secs)	5.8	5.2
Fuel economy (mpg)	29	26
Desirability	★ ★ ★ ★	
Availability	★ ★ ★ ★ ★	
Tuneability	★ ★ ★ ★ ★	

Cosworth standing. *Autocar* recorded a top speed of 137mph and a remarkable 0-60mph time of just 5.8 seconds, which the magazine described as "scarcely believable."

Very quickly a waiting list developed as Colin McRae stormed to victory in the World Rally Championship. At its peak, the Turbo would account for an incredible 65 per cent of Impreza sales in the UK.

A facelifted model was launched in October 1996 featuring a new-look sportier exterior with a deeply contoured bonnet line. The interior grew plusher and the dreadful cloth seats were replaced by high-backed winged sports front seats. Under-bonnet improvements boosted torque from 201lb ft (270Nm) to 214lb ft (290Nm) at lower revs. The gearbox was also slicker-acting and there was a new, thicker rear anti-roll bar.

October 1997 saw a major overhaul of the interior with a completely new dashboard featuring white dials, a lidded box and twin airbags. Further changes

Early Impreza interiors were pretty basic. This 1998 Terzo cabin has improved seats and dials.

The Impreza Turbo must have been a highly effective police car. You'd think twice about trying to outrun this!

in October 1998 included bigger brakes, four-pot front brake calipers, ventilated rear discs, a taller STi type rear wing and new seats. More significant was a new Phase 2 version of the EJ20 engine that yielded an extra 7PS (up to 218PS).

Special editions were truly special, too. The first was the 1995 Series McRae with its gold alloys, retrimmed interior, and McRae-signed Recaro seats. Then came the 1997 Catalunya and the 1998 Terzo, then the 1999 RB5 with its 17-inch alloys and stiffer bodyshell, which could be had with an optional Prodrive Performance Pack boosting power to 240PS.

It is worth briefly mentioning the USA, where the "hot" Impreza was called the RS. Launched for the 1998 model year, it had a 2.5-litre normally-aspirated engine with a disappointing 165PS on tap, although it certainly looked the part.

The Impreza Turbo makes one of the most convincing used car buys around. Owners rave about its reliability and durability – it scored first place in the JD Power customer satisfaction survey – and depreciation is less crushing than many rivals. That said, cars have often been thrashed so you need to be careful in your checks, and Imprezas require meticulous servicing, which can be expensive.

Brakes take a pounding and discs can last as little as 20,000 miles. Bent or new rear suspension links and distorted inner front wishbone mounts indicate accident damage or serious kerbing.

The flat-four engine has a sound all of its own but the turbo should be quiet and there should be no smoke from the exhaust at idle. Replacing a turbocharger is costly, as is the cambelt, which needs changing every 45,000 miles. The 4x4 system is an extremely tough item but check for a notchy gearchange, while clutches are very costly to replace.

SUBARU IMPREZA
WRX 1992-2000

The letters WRX meant absolutely nothing when Subaru launched its turbocharged 4x4 mid-sized Impreza in Japan. They came to mean a hell of a lot across the whole world – despite the fact that the WRX badge was kept in Japan for the first eight year of its life.

It all began in 1992 with the first WRX. This may have looked similar to the later European Turbo but its flat-four EJ20 engine was a lot more powerful, thanks to a larger turbocharger and intercooler, run by a different engine management set-up. Rated by the Japanese measuring system it came in at 240PS, although that rose to 260PS for 1994 and to 280PS in 1996. Power was not the only difference over export Turbos: the suspension was stiffer, climate control was standard, the mirrors were electrically retractable, and there were standard rear wash/wipers even on the saloon. Also the saloon – the only WRX body style available at launch – did not come with the folding rear seat of the European Turbo, having a solid rear bulkhead instead.

Also available from 1992 launch was a lightweight RA version, which made do without numerous items of equipment (no foglamps or boot spoiler, for example). Conforming to a Japanese penchant for stripped-out rally-style lightweight models, the RA would make a consistent appearance in Subaru's catalogues in a bewildering array of types. All RA engines prior to 1996 featured a "closed-deck" block, which made the engine much more amenable to modification, while the RA's gearing was also shorter.

SPECIFICATION	WRX saloon	WRX Sports Wagon
Engine	1994cc flat-four	1994cc flat-four
Max power	240PS @ 6000rpm (260PS from 1994/280PS from 1996)	220PS @ 6000rpm (240PS from 1996/250PS from 1997)
Torque	224lb ft (304Nm) @ 5000rpm (later 242lb ft (328Nm) at 4000rpm)	206lb ft (280Nm) @ 5000rpm (later 225lb ft (306Nm) @ 4000rpm)
Transmission	5-speed manual	5-speed manual or 4-speed automatic
Brakes	Vented disc/solid disc	Vented disc/solid disc
Length/Width/Height	4340/1690/1400mm	4340/1690/1435mm
Weight	1230kg (RA 1080kg)	1300kg (SA 1250kg)
PERFORMANCE		
Max speed (mph)	140	140
0-60mph (secs)	5.0	5.1
Fuel economy (mpg)	28	28
Desirability	★ ★ ★ ★ ★	
Availability	★ ★ ★ ★	
Tuneability	★ ★ ★ ★ ★	

The WRX Sports Wagon five-door launched in 1993 had a detuned engine of "only" 220PS (raised to 250PS in 1997 and a year later falling back to 240PS). The five-door also came in a lightweight version called the SA that skimmed 50kg off the overall weight. Another peculiarity was a WRX version with four-speed automatic transmission.

The manual-transmission WRX has always been the most civilised of the Japanese Impreza family to drive, thanks to a more forgiving set of gear ratios and a higher final drive ratio than more senior WRX

Japan's Impreza WRX had more power and more equipment than export Turbos.

The heart of the WRX was its intercooled, turbocharged flat-four engine.

models, but even this was considerably more buzzy than the EU-spec Impreza Turbo.

As a grey import, the WRX is commonly seen, if slightly eclipsed by the STi. It can make a great entry-level Impreza buy, as the WRX tends to be cheaper than the STi but quicker and better equipped than a Turbo. Japanese cars were not undersealed from new, so require extra checking for rust, while accident damage is common. Don't expect much service history, which means you'll be taking more of a risk, while many cars have been modified.

SUBARU IMPREZA
WRX STi 1994-2000

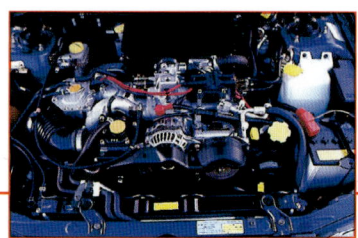

280PS from the STi engine made it the enthusiast's choice.

The three letters "STi" transformed the Impreza WRX into "the real thing." STi is a moniker for Subaru Tecnica International, the company's rally and tuning wing. Arriving in 1994, the Impreza STi's specification began to approach that of the world rally Impreza.

Power was boosted, initially to 250PS but soon after up to the maximum allowed by Japanese custom, 280PS. Each engine was blueprinted and added a red cylinder clock, forged pistons, bigger valves, a better intercooler, a bigger radiator and an uprated turbocharger. It revved higher too – up to 8250rpm, some 750rpm higher than the WRX – and the exhaust had a much wider bore.

Equally significant was the STi's gearbox. Rebuilt with closer ratios and a quicker shift action, it was allied to a lower (4.444:1) final drive. The result was devastating in-gear performance and more durable internals. The STi was a genuine 150mph car with supercar-slaying acceleration: how about 0-60mph in 4.6 seconds and a 50-70mph time of under three seconds?

As for the suspension, aluminium lower front wishbones were supplemented by a carbon-fibre strut brace. Also the brakes were much stronger thanks to four-pot front calipers and ventilated rear discs, while there was a wide range of accessories and tuning parts available direct from STi.

You could spot an STi by the details. The foglamps were replaced by blank panels bearing the STi logo, there was a tall rear spoiler, pink front grille badge, gold alloy wheels and an aluminium bonnet and boot lid. Yet the STi was no stripped-out special, with standard climate control, remote central locking, electric windows and driver airbag, while the rally-style seats had suede inserts. You could buy an STi in four-door saloon or five-door estate forms, both with identical mechanical specifications.

The Impreza STi went through evolutions on a virtually annual basis. It started with the Version I in 1994, basically a factory-modified special. The 1995 Version II was the first to appear officially in company literature. The 1996 Version III was the facelift model and the first with 280PS – and cited by Subaru's engineering chief as his favourite Impreza of all. The 1997 Version IV got a mild torque boost, the 1998 Version V got a bigger rear spoiler and new spotlamp covers, while the final Version VI got an uprated clutch. You may also come across one of many sought-after limited edition models, usually bearing the name "V-Limited" and usually painted in rally-livery blue. There was also a very wild run-out S201 special edition with 300PS, a major bodykit and a massive rear spoiler.

Pink badges and foglamp covers betray the ultra-focused Impreza WRX STi.

To many eyes, however, the regular STi is the best all-round Impreza of all. Not only is it exceptionally fast but its suspension and transmission retain a useable balance for road use that is lost in more extreme Imprezas.

Speaking of which, the STi Type R definitely represented an Impreza extreme. The Type R was unique in that it was sold as a two-door coupe that resembled the rally Impreza with its extended front spoiler, side skirts and deeper rear valance. The Type R also gained a pukka Group N gearbox that gave it even closer gear ratios and a final drive equating to just 19mph at 1000rpm. Top speed and motorway cruising were adversely affected but that was never the point of the Type R. This was a car for pure acceleration and one for anyone who loves shifting gears a lot.

The other major Type R changes were a centre differential that could be altered by the driver, a limited slip differential on the front axle replacing ABS, a mechanical differential rather than the viscous-coupled one of the "ordinary" Imprezas, a quick ratio steering rack and a water spray for the intercooler. There was also an STi Type RA, essentially the four-door STi saloon with the Type R stripped-out spec (easily recognisable by its roof-mounted air vent).

There is no doubt that enthusiasts view the STi as the "genuine article". It is the pinnacle of the Impreza breed and if you find a good example of the "classic" shape STi, you will have what many regard as the most focused Impreza of all. It is extremely fast, has the most developed suspension and brakes and looks the most aggressive too.

As the STi was never officially imported to Europe, every example will be a grey import. That means that any car with a long service history is worth a strong premium – it's definitely a more risky buy with a patchy history. Many examples have been thrashed or modified, so it pays to get it thoroughly checked over by someone who knows these cars.

The two-door STi Type R was even closer to Subaru's WRC rally car.

SPECIFICATION		
	STi	**STi Type R**
Engine	1994cc flat-four	1994cc flat-four
Max power	250PS @ 6000rpm (280PS @ 6500rpm from 1996)	280PS @ 6500rpm
Torque	228lb ft (309Nm) @ 5000rpm (253lb ft (343Nm) @ 4000rpm from 1996)	260lb ft (352Nm) @ 4000rpm
Transmission	5-speed manual	5-speed manual
Brakes	Vented disc/vented disc	Vented disc/vented disc
Length/Width/Height	4340/1690/1400mm	4340/1690/1400mm
Weight	1300kg (RA 1260kg)	1260kg
PERFORMANCE		
Max speed (mph)	150	150
0-60mph (secs)	4.6	4.4
Fuel economy (mpg)	24	23
Desirability	✱ ✱ ✱ ✱ ✱	
Availability	✱ ✱ ✱ ✱	
Tuneability	✱ ✱ ✱ ✱ ✱	

SUBARU IMPREZA
WRX STi 22B 1998

Wide-track chassis, blistered arches and an expanded engine marked out the Impreza STi 22B.

The ultimate production Impreza is probably the phenomenal 22B, a limited edition made in 1998 only. The two-door STi Type R body went on a course of steroids (designed by McLaren F1 man Peter Stevens), resulting in an even deeper front spoiler, big wheel arch blisters and side skirts, while the adjustable rear spoiler was an exact replica of the WRC car.

Underneath bristled a unique chassis with wider forged-aluminium suspension arms, massive 17-inch gold alloy wheels and wide tyres. An adjustable centre differential, heavy-duty close-ratio gearbox, twin-plate clutch, uprated brakes and extremely firm springing completed a serious driver's chassis.

But the most crucial part of the 22B was its larger flat-four engine, up from 1997cc to 2212cc. Subaru said the power output remained unchanged at 280PS but rumours persisted of outputs well in excess of 300PS, and there was a driver-operated water-spray for the intercooler.

Magazine testers were agreed that the 22B was an animal to pilot. In all respects it boasted knife-sharp responses: super-sensitive steering, biting clutch action, hugely powerful non-ABS brakes, ultra-grippy tyres and a completely lag-free turbo. Frankly frantic to drive, the 22B was the car that really got you to feel like McRae. A plaque inside the car informed you that only 400 had been made (actually 424 were built), 16 of which were modified and imported to the UK officially as the Type UK, many more unofficially.

SPECIFICATION	
Engine	2212cc flat-four
Max power	280PS @ 6000rpm
Torque	265lb ft @ 3200rpm
Transmission	5-speed manual
Brakes	Vented disc/vented disc
Length/Width/Height	4340/1770/1400mm
Weight	1270kg
PERFORMANCE	
Max speed (mph)	140
0-60mph (secs)	4.6
Fuel economy (mpg)	20
Desirability	✱ ✱ ✱ ✱ ✱
Availability	✱
Tuneability	✱ ✱ ✱ ✱ ✱

SUBARU IMPREZA

P1 1999-2000

In 1999 Subaru UK enlisted Prodrive's help to create a fully European type-approved version of the two-door STi Type R. To answer the challenge of the grey imports, the P1 (Prodrive One) got the same 280PS power output yet was fully emissions compliant. With its 155mph top speed and 0-60 in 4.6 seconds, the P1 was one of the quickest of all Imprezas.

The P1 was less raw to drive than the Type R and more in tune with European tastes, thanks to carefully tuned wheel and tyre sizes and spring, damper and anti-roll bar rates, including Peter Stevens-designed 10-spoke OZ 17-inch wheels and lower Prodrive/Eibach springs.

Peter Stevens also designed new front and rear spoilers, while the only colour offered was Sonic Blue with blue Alcantara interior trim. The P1 was only sold in the UK – a total of 1000 examples.

Although the P1 was blisteringly quick, there was some criticism of the soft front suspension and brakes. A P1 WR package was therefore offered with 18-inch OZ alloy wheels, uprated brakes, better exhaust and Prodrive Recaro seats. It had a harder ride but better handling and is today highly sought-after.

The P1 (Prodrive One) was only available in Sonic Blue with blue Alcantara trim.

SPECIFICATION

Engine	1994cc flat-four
Max power	280PS @ 6500rpm
Torque	260lb ft (352Nm) @ 4000rpm
Transmission	5-speed manual
Brakes	Vented disc/vented disc
Length/Width/Height	4340/1690/1400mm
Weight	1275kg

PERFORMANCE

Max speed (mph)	155
0-60mph (secs)	4.6
Fuel economy (mpg)	23
Desirability	★ ★ ★ ★ ★
Availability	★ ★
Tuneability	★ ★ ★ ★ ★

SUBARU IMPREZA
WRX 2000-date

Controversy surrounded the New Age Impreza's headlamp design.

SUBARU IMPREZA WRX 2000-DATE

With the new WRX came a major upgrade in interior quality, along with a new fascia design.

After around 730,000 classic-shape Imprezas had been made, in August 2000 Subaru launched the "New Age" Impreza. It was comprehensively restyled and a little larger in all dimensions. There were now much more marked styling differences between the four and five-door variants. The saloon had a wider track, which meant prominently blistered wheel arches that were lacking on the five-door.

But all media attention focused on one thing: round headlamps that many compared to a Toyota Celica. Controversy reigned: Subaru was adamant it had got it right but everyone else knew they looked gawky, and Subaru did eventually cave in, restyling them within two years.

Under the skin, the new Impreza did not deviate from the time-honoured formula. The new shell was, however, much stiffer than before. The suspension struts and wheel hub assemblies moved 10mm outward and the rear roll centre was raised by 33mm. A new front subframe and stronger cross member connections reduced noise, while forged aluminium lower arms were now standard across the board. Steering was improved and there were standard four-pot front brake callipers.

The EJ20 turbo engine was only mildly reworked. As before, the full-time all-wheel drive transmission had a 50/50 front/rear torque split, varying to changing conditions. There remained a centre differential with viscous coupling and a limited slip differential in the rear axle to apportion grip between each rear wheel.

A massive upgrade in interior quality was very

SUBARU IMPREZA WRX 2000-DATE

The EJ20 turbo engine was only mildly reworked for the 2000 WRX. Power was up to 225PS from 218.

For the first time, the five-door had a narrower track than the four-door. This is a 2005 model.

welcome, as was a new fascia design and silver-finish centre panel. Interior space was better too.

European models had 17-inch wheels and a 218PS engine, plus standard ABS, CD, central locking and air conditioning. Japanese cars had 250PS thanks to a larger turbo and intercooler. You also had the option of automatic transmission in Japan.

Opinion was divided over whether the new WRX was better to drive. The engine was torquier and refinement much better but some of the pace and sharpness had been worn away.

Faced with almost universal criticism of the Impreza's headlamp treatment, Subaru gave it a completely fresh front end for 2003: new front bumper, spoiler, bonnet and wings, plus new headlamps and rear lights. Power rose from 218PS up to 225PS so it was quicker too. The steering and damping were made sportier, while a new luxury SL package included leather seats and a sunroof. For 2005, the WRX improved again, with a sort of diluted STi chassis (inverted struts, aluminium lateral links and STi steering revisions).

One footnote is the UK300 limited edition of 2001, featuring Peter Stevens body mods (black gloss headlamp shells, extended front spoiler and quirkily droopy rear aerofoil), plus enormous gold OZ 18-inch alloys. Only 300 were made, some with an optional 245PS Prodrive Performance Pack.

SPECIFICATION		
	WRX (Europe)	**WRX (Japan)**
Engine	1994cc flat-four	1994cc flat-four
Max power	218PS @ 5600rpm (225PS @ 6500rpm from 2003)	250PS @ 6000rpm
Torque	215lb ft (292Nm) @ 3600rpm (221lb ft (300Nm) @ 4000rpm from 2003)	245lb ft (332Nm) @ 3600rpm
Transmission	5-speed manual	5-speed manual or 4-speed automatic
Brakes	Vented disc/vented disc	Vented disc/vented disc
Length/Width/Height	4405/1730/1440mm	4405/1730/1440mm
Weight	1385kg (estate 1410kg)	1340kg (estate 1370kg)
PERFORMANCE		
Max speed (mph)	140	140
0-60mph (secs)	5.7	5.3
Fuel economy (mpg)	30	28
Desirability	★★★★	
Availability	★★★★★	
Tuneability	★★★★★	

SUBARU IMPREZA
WRX STi 2000-date

Finally Subaru brought the WRX STi to Europe. This is a facelifted 2005 model.

Grip was improved in 2005 by the fitment of Bridgestone Potenza tyres on wider 8x17 gold alloys.

The New Age STi, launched in Japan in October 2000, continued the tradition of the butch near-rally spec Impreza. The difference was, it would eventually make it to Europe and elsewhere in an official capacity for the first time.

The Japanese STi continued with the full 280PS but its torque was also considerably up at 275lb ft (373Nm) thanks to a bigger turbo and different mapping. Undoubtedly the single most important addition was an all-new six-speed close-ratio gearbox fitted alongside a Suretrac front limited slip differential (rather than a free diff). Body rigidity was improved as were the wishbones, springs and dampers. Brembo brakes (gold coloured) were ventilated front and rear. In Japan there was also a five-door STi as well as the more popular

In 2004 Subaru produced this WR1 special edition in the UK with a 320PS engine.

four-door, both of which were 100kg heavier than the old STi.

As before, there was a lightweight STi Type RA weighing some 30kg less. Other RA differences were a quicker steering rack, harder suspension, roof ventilator, no ABS or air con, white-only colour scheme and a driver-controlled centre differential.

Then in December 2001 came the STi RA Spec C. This was no less than 90kg lighter than the standard STi and it also got a 22B turbo, revised cylinders and intake manifold to boost response and torque. The Spec C also rode 10mm lower than the STi. The S202 edition of 2002 was based on Spec C but its power rose to 320PS; 2005's S203 had the same 320PS output plus 18-inch alloys and a restyled nose.

The STi finally made it to Europe in early 2002. 95 per cent the same as the Jap-spec STi, it had a pukka STi engine, though an extra catalyst and remapping dropped power by 15PS to 265PS. A Prodrive Performance Pack, boasting 305PS at 6000rpm, was an extremely popular option in the UK.

The UK STi got smoked glass HID headlamps, air con, CD and satellite tracking. As well as the "normal" STi, a Prodrive Style version was initially offered, boasting a bigger WRC-style rear wing, restyled front spoiler and blue-faced dials.

Like the WRX, the STi was facelifted in 2002. But the 2005 model year saw major changes: the wheelbase grew by 10mm and the rear track by 15mm. The geometry and suspension settings were also altered, as

Cockpit of the 2003 STi.

well as the steering. A helical limited-slip front differential replaced the Suretrac diff. Two new pieces of equipment finally matched the Mitsubishi Evo: a yaw sensor to detect the rate of drift, and a driver-controlled centre differential (DCCD). Grip was also enhanced by Bridgestone Potenza tyres on wider 17x8 gold alloys (which necessitated small blisters on the rear wheel-larches). The cabin looked and felt better too.

It's worth mentioning the UK-only WR1 of 2004, which featured a 320PS power upgrade and a driver control centre differential, plus uprated springs, a 25mm lower ride height and 18-inch wheels.

In the USA, the STi was launched in 2003 with a very different engine: 2.5 litres, not 2.0 litres. Developing 300PS, Subaru was able to claim it to be the most powerful four-cylinder engine available in the USA. The 2.5-litre STi engine block has become very popular with UK tuners, who have discovered it in a big way.

SPECIFICATION		
	STi (Europe)	STi WR1 (UK only)
Engine	1994cc flat-four	1994cc flat-four
Max power	265PS @ 6000rpm	320PS @ 5800rpm
Torque	253lb ft (343Nm) @ 4000rpm	310lb ft (420Nm) @ 4000rpm
Transmission	6-speed manual	6-speed manual
Brakes	Vented disc/vented disc	Vented disc/vented disc
Length/Width/Height	4405/1730/1440mm	4405/1730/1440mm
Weight	1470kg	1470kg
PERFORMANCE		
Max speed (mph)	152	155
0-60mph (secs)	5.2	4.25
Fuel economy (mpg)	25	23
Desirability	★ ★ ★ ★ ★	
Availability	★ ★ ★ ★	
Tuneability	★ ★ ★ ★ ★	

SUBARU IMPREZA WRX 2000-DATE

SPECIFICATION

	STi (Japan)	STi RA Spec C (Japan)	STi (USA)
Engine	1994cc flat-four	1994cc flat-four	2457cc flat-four
Max power	280PS @ 6400rpm	280-320PS @ 6400rpm	300PS @ 6000rpm
Torque	275lb ft (373Nm) @ 4000rpm (304lb ft (412Nm) from Sep 2004)	283lb ft (385Nm) @ 4400rpm (304lb ft (412Nm) from Sep 2004)	300lb ft (407Nm) @ 4000rpm
Transmission	6-speed manual	6-speed manual	6-speed manual
Brakes	Vented disc/vented disc	Vented disc/vented disc	Vented disc/vented disc
Length/Width/Height	4405/1730/1440mm	4405/1730/1440mm	4405/1730/1440mm
Weight	1400kg (RA 1370kg)	1310kg	1483kg

PERFORMANCE

Max speed (mph)	155	155	155
0-60mph (secs)	4.9	4.6	4.8
Fuel economy (mpg)	23	23	23
Desirability	* * * * *		
Availability	* * *		
Tuneability	* * * * *		

In Japan the STi engine produced 280PS as opposed to only 265PS in European spec. A Prodrive performance pack could take power to 305PS.

SUBARU FORESTER
S-TURBO & tb 1997-2002

The Forester had genuine off-road ability, aided by its 200mm gorund clearance.

Based on the Impreza floorpan, the Forester S-Turbo was a surprisingly quick 4x4.

When Subaru launched the Forester, it effectively created its own niche: an estate/4x4 cross-over with a sporty flavour. European markets got an S-Turbo model, boasting engine and suspension derived from the Impreza Turbo. That made it rapid, agile and sure-footed – an undiscovered gem. It also had genuine off-road credentials with its useful 200mm (7.8-inch) ground clearance. However, with only 170PS on tap (later 177PS), it was nowhere near the Impreza in terms of performance. The USA fared even worse, with a mere 150bhp from a 2.5-litre engine.

One Japanese market Forester did have Impreza-crushing pace – the tb, launched in 1998. Its EJ20 flat-four engine was identical to the Impreza WRX's, producing 240PS. The tb may have been a little heavier than the Impreza, but it got the lower final drive of the WRX STi, which makes up the acceleration shortfall. 0-60 in 6.4 seconds makes it a very quick car. A four-speed automatic transmission was an alternative to the five-speed manual.

Two tb versions were offered in initially: the S/tb and well-equipped T/tb adding a rear spoiler, CD and side airbags. Other versions followed, including the Type A model ("Aero" spoilers, gold alloys and leather seats) and an STi-badged version, which had lower suspension. The Forester got a minor facelift in 2000.

SPECIFICATION

	tb (Japan)	S-Turbo (Europe)
Engine	1994cc flat-four	1994cc flat-four
Max power	240-250PS @ 6000rpm	170-177PS @ 5600rpm
Torque	228lb ft (309Nm) @ 5000rpm	177lb ft (240Nm) @ 3200rpm
Transmission	5-speed manual or 4-speed auto	5-speed manual or 4-speed auto
Brakes	Vented disc/solid disc	Vented disc/solid disc
Length/Width/Height	4450/1735/1580mm	4450/1735/1580mm
Weight	1390kg	1420kg

PERFORMANCE

Max speed (mph)	140	123
0-60mph (secs)	6.4	8.2
Fuel economy (mpg)	21	28
Desirability	* * *	
Availability	* * *	*
Tuneability	* * *	*

SUBARU FORESTER

XT & STi 2002-date

Second generation Forester hardly different to the first. This is the powerful 2.5 XT version.

You could be excused for not realising there ever was a second generation Forester, since it looked so much like the first one. The front end looked more aggressive with its deep grille, recessed foglamps and multi-bulb headlamps, while the rear end was restyled too.

Both front and rear tracks grew, resulting in blistered wheelarches. Improvements included better fuel economy and aerodynamics, greater engine and transmission refinement, sharper handling, enhanced safety, and extra interior room.

The new Forester won the 2003 Japanese Car of the Year award, and thankfully there remained a Turbo model, now called the 2.0 XT, with 177PS. The true performance model arrived in 2004, when European markets received a new 2.5-litre XT. Its 211PS engine got a semi-closed deck cylinder block, strengthened pistons and connecting rods, sodium-filled hollow exhaust valves and hollow camshafts. The 2.5 XT also got a rear limited-slip differential and self-levelling rear suspension.

Also in Japan there was a Forester STi with the EJ25 2.5-litre engine but tuned up to 265PS, coupled with the Impreza six-speed manual gearbox, lower and tougher suspension, quicker steering, Brembo brakes and a special STi interior.

SPECIFICATION				
	2.0 XT (EU)	**2.5 XT (EU)**	**2.0 XT (Japan)**	**STi (Japan)**
Engine	1994cc flat-four	2457cc flat-four	1994cc flat-four	2457cc flat-four
Max power	177PS @ 5600rpm	211PS @ 5600rpm	220PS @ 6000rpm	265PS @ 5600rpm
Torque	181lb ft (245Nm) @ 3200rpm	236lb ft @ 3600rpm	228lb ft (309Nm) @ 5000rpm	279lb ft (378Nm) @ 3600rpm
Transmission	5-sp man or 4-sp auto	5-sp man	5-sp man or 4-sp auto	6-sp man
Brakes	Vented disc/solid disc	Vented disc/solid disc	Vented disc/solid disc	Vented disc/solid disc
Length/Width/Height	4450/1735/1580mm	4450/1735/1580mm	4450/1735/1580mm	4450/1735/1580mm
Weight	1430kg	1430kg	1430kg	1430kg
PERFORMANCE				
Max speed (mph)	121	140	140	145
0-60mph (secs)	7.9	6.0	6.0	5.8
Fuel economy (mpg)	29	25	25	23
Desirability	*	*	*	
Availability	*	*	*	*
Tuneability	*	*	*	*

SUBARU LEGACY
RS & GT-B 1993-1998

Four-wheel drive and 280PS for the big Legacy RS. This is a 1993 saloon.

Subaru's Legacy was first launched in 1989 and was an absolute landmark model. Designed by Giugiaro, its platform would serve for ten years in two generations of Legacy, while it also formed the basis for the Impreza and Forester. The trademark Subaru boxer four-cylinder engine was there, also in turbocharged RS versions in Japan, forming the basis of Subaru's rally effort. The RS Turbo got a centre differential with viscous coupling.

The Legacy was updated in 1993 and, while the RS still never arrived in Britain, drivers got used to its performance credentials with the Legacy 4cam which had 200PS. The Japanese super-Legacies – badged RS and GT-B – had no less than 280PS and impressive cornering powers.

The flat-four engine had the same 1994cc capacity as the Impreza but it was a quite different unit. Most notably it had twin turbochargers rather than a single one. Its 280PS was, compared to the Impreza, delivered usefully further down the rev range, making it a more relaxed drive. There were also slightly less incisive GT saloon and estate models with 260bhp and four-speed automatic transmission – great choices if you want practicality and performance with the extra convenience of automatic transmission.

The saloon version was called the RS and the estate the GT-B – the "B" stands for Bilstein, who provided the gas dampers in the uprated suspension package. The estate was a more popular choice with its huge load capacity – up to 1645 litres with the seats folded.

For such a complete car, used prices start surprisingly low. When buying used, you need to be sure that the car you're offered is a genuine GT-B, not one of the lesser Legacies, such as the non-turbo 250T or the bizarrely-named Brighton-Gold or Lancaster.

SPECIFICATION	
Engine	1994cc flat-four
Max power	280PS @ 6500rpm (260PS on GT)
Torque	253lb ft (343Nm) @ 5000rpm
Transmission	5-sp man (4-sp auto on GT)
Brakes	Disc/disc
Length/Width/Height	4605/1695/1405mm
Weight	1410kg (RS), 1480kg (GT-B)
PERFORMANCE	
Max speed (mph)	155
0-60mph (secs)	6.1
Fuel economy (mpg)	20
Desirability	✶ ✶ ✶
Availability	✶ ✶
Tuneability	✶ ✶ ✶ ✶

SUBARU LEGACY
RSK-B4 & GT-B 1998-2003

In Japan a version was marketed under the Blitzen name.

Second generation Legacy was far more sophisticated. This is a 1999 RSK-B4.

The Japanese Blitzen version came with this rather adventurous interior.

The 1998-2003 generation Legacy marked a big improvement, perhaps the biggest leap forward being the interior. Compared to the old Legacy and Impreza, it was a finely-finished, neatly-styled, quality cabin featuring sports seats, a Momo leather steering wheel, clear dials and chunky switchgear. There was plenty of equipment, too, including electric seats, climate control and a CD player.

No less an engineering company than Porsche tweaked Subaru's family saloon chassis to create the Legacy RSK-B4 (which was the saloon version), while the estate continued as the GT-B. In four-door saloon form it could seat five adults comfortably, while in GT-B estate guise it was a load swallower that few cars could beat.

A very similar flat-four twin-turbo engine still pumped out 280PS and plenty of torque thanks to twin sequential turbochargers (one a light pressure unit adding useful torque up to 4500rpm, the other letting rip up to the 7500rpm red line). A less powerful 260PS engine was fitted to automatic transmission cars.

Add in the raw statistics of its performance – 157mph and 0-60 in under six seconds – and you have a practical supercar that is even faster than the Mitsubishi Galant VR-4. For such a complete car, used prices start surprisingly low, making this one of the undiscovered jewels of Japan.

SPECIFICATION

Engine	1994cc flat-four
Max power	280PS @ 6500rpm (260PS with auto)
Torque	249lb ft (338Nm) @ 5000rpm
	(235lb ft (319Nm) with auto)
Transmission	5-sp man or 4-sp auto
Brakes	Vented disc/solid disc
Length/Width/Height	4605/1695/1410mm
Weight	1380kg (saloon), 1450kg (estate)

PERFORMANCE

Max speed (mph)	157
0-60mph (secs)	5.9
Fuel economy (mpg)	20
Desirability	★ ★ ★
Availability	★ ★ ★
Tuneability	★ ★ ★ ★

SUBARU LEGACY
B4 & 3.0R 2003-date

Third generation Legacy made it to Europe as the more focused 3.0R spec.B.

The Legacy 3.0R spec.B Sports Tourer was a super-swift load carrier.

The third-generation Legacy was launched in 2003 to widespread acclaim: it was far less soft than before, more European in flavour and won the Car of the Year Japan Award 2003-2004. In Japan there continued to be a hot B4 edition. This continued with the 280PS EJ20 2.0 turbo engine, now tuned with extra torque, and available in saloon, estate, manual and automatic versions.

There was now a new 3.0R model with a 245PS flat six-cylinder EZ30 engine, still driving all four wheels. Lavishly equipped, in the UK it boasted electric front seats, 6CD system, electric sunroof and satellite navigation. It was however, more of an executive express than a true performance model.

From 2004 that role fell to the new spec.B model that was added in European markets, featuring an Impreza STi-based six-speed manual gearbox, uprated suspension with front inverted struts, Bilstein dampers and larger 18-inch wheels. It was also available as a saloon or Sports Tourer estate, each with subtly upgraded body styling and a special leather interior. It was rapid and refined but still could not be compared to the Impreza for sporty feel.

SPECIFICATION

	B4	3.0R
Engine	1994cc flat-four	2999cc flat-six
Max power	280PS @ 6400rpm (260PS with auto)	245PS @ 6000rpm
Torque	253lb ft (343Nm) @ 2400rpm	219lb ft (297Nm) @ 4400rpm
Transmission	5-sp man or 5-sp auto	5-sp man or 5-sp auto (Spec B 6-sp)
Brakes	Vented disc/vented disc	Vented disc/vented disc
Length/Width/Height	4635/1730/1425mm (saloon), 4680/1730/1470mm (estate)	
Weight	1410kg	1470kg

PERFORMANCE

Max speed (mph)	157	151
0-60mph (secs)	6.0	6.5
Fuel economy (mpg)	20	28
Desirability	* * *	
Availability	* * *	
Tuneability	* * * *	

SUZUKI

100PS Suzuki Swift GTi could do 0-60mph in 8.7 seconds and reach 114mph.

Miniature Suzuki Cappuccino weighed just 700kg and had a 658cc turbocharged three-cylinder engine.

Suzuki is better known for its motorbikes than its cars. Even within its car range, it does city-sized microcars best (indeed it is the leading Japanese maker of so-called K-cars). But performance cars? Actually, yes. While they're not Skylines, Suzuki's pocket-sized performers are miniature GTIs and even sports cars.

The first car to garner any reputation outside Japan was the **Swift GTI**. As a competition car it was effective in small engine classes and as a road car it was crude but effective. It was first seen in 1987, sporting a 1.3-litre 16-valve fuel-injected twin-cam engine with 100bhp. Priced so low, it offered a sensational power-to-weight ratio. It could do 0-60mph in 8.7 seconds and reach 114mph, with above average handling. The GTI finally ducked out of production in 1996.

By then Suzuki had introduced the **Cappuccino**, a frothy miniature sports car. Only 3.3 metres long, it was ultra-lightweight (700kg), enabling its 658cc turbocharged three-cylinder engine to deliver sharp performance. Expect 0-60mph in under 10 seconds and a top speed of 110mph – although tuners have extracted amazing figures from the pint-pot sportster. The front engine/rear drive layout dished up amazing ability with superb grip and balance. A semi-exotic spec included a limited slip differential, double wishbone front and multi-link rear suspension, power-assisted steering and disc brakes all round (the front set being ventilated).

The Cappuccino's party piece was its clever roof arrangement, a four-piece folding hard top. There were two targa panels, each of which could be removed for T-bar motoring. Then you could take out the central bar (stowing everything in the boot) and drop the solid rear section away out of sight. Criticisms? A narrow cockpit, lack of legroom, choppy ride and high noise levels.

Another micro-sports car was the **Cara** – basically a rebadged version of the Mazda AZ-1, a 658cc mid-engined gullwing coupe with easily removable plastic body panels.

The final Suzuki of note is the **Alto Works**, the hot version of the tiny Alto city car. Not sold outside Japan, it is little known, but it's been on sale in various generations since 1987, always featuring a turbocharged three-cylinder 658cc engine and a choice of front- or four-wheel drive.

TOYOTA
STARLET
GT TURBO 1986-1996

Turbocharged cars came into their own in the 1980s and one of the most surprising of all was Toyota's Starlet GT Turbo. This may have been a classic case of sow's ear (the normal Starlet was good at supermarkets and little else) but the turbo in such a small car produced peppy performance.

The first Starlet GT Turbo arrived in 1986 sporting a tiny 1296cc fuel-injected 12-valve engine with a single turbo and oil cooler. Despite its meagre 105PS output, weighing only 770kg helped its cause and it delivered a violent punch.

The best generation was the 1989-1996 one with its bigger 1331cc 16-valve engine and intercooled turbo – good for 135PS and 0-60 in 6.9 seconds. Actually it had a two-mode turbo allowing the driver to change boost levels (low mode had 125PS). There was a third GT Turbo (1996-1999) but this was heavier and slower.

Sadly the GT Turbo was a Japan-only model. The quickest Starlet sold in the UK was the SR, which had a mere 76PS.

SPECIFICATION

	1986-1989	1989-1996
Engine	1296cc 4-cyl	1331cc 4-cyl
Max power	105PS @ 5600rpm	135PS @ 6400rpm
Torque	110lb ft (149Nm) @ 3600rpm	116lb ft (157Nm) @ 4800rpm
Transmission	5-speed manual	5-speed manual
Brakes	Vented disc/solid disc	Vented disc/solid disc
Length/Width/Height	3700/1590/1395mm	3800/1620/1380mm
Weight	770kg	830kg

PERFORMANCE

Max speed (mph)	119	124
0-60mph (secs)	8.1	6.9
Fuel economy (mpg)	39	37
Desirability	*	*
Availability	*	*
Tuneability	*	*

An underrated performance pocket rocket: the Toyota Starlet GT Turbo.

TOYOTA COROLLA
GT 1984-1987

Front-drive Corolla GT of 1984 was one of Japan's first-ever hot hatches.

While old-school enthusiasts drooled over the rear-drive Corolla AE86, the new school was represented by the AE82 series front-wheel drive Corolla launched at the same time.

While the ordinary Corolla of 1983 was dull, the GT version launched in 1984 was a real performance car – and one of the very first Japanese hot hatches. Unlike the AE86, its engine was the 4AGE 1.6-litre twin-cam, driving through a five-speed gearbox to the front wheels.

This first-generation front-drive Corolla was a fairly feisty car for its day and has a small following now, although it remains overshadowed by the contemporary Corolla AE86. It's very cheap to buy and not that expensive to keep going, although rust is a problem you have to keep on top of.

SPECIFICATION	
Engine	1587cc 4-cyl
Max power	120PS @ 6600rpm
Torque	103lb ft (140Nm) @ 5000rpm
Transmission	5-speed manual
Brakes	Disc/disc
Length/Width/Height	3970/1656/1379mm
Weight	950kg
PERFORMANCE	
Max speed (mph)	121
0-60mph (secs)	8.5
Fuel economy (mpg)	33
Desirability	★ ★
Availability	★ ★
Tuneability	★ ★

TOYOTA
COROLLA
AE86/LEVIN/TRUENO 1983-1987

Enthusiasts still adore the AE86 Corolla GT coupé with its agile rear-wheel drive handling.

SPECIFICATION
Engine	1587cc 4-cyl
Max power	125PS @ 6600rpm (130PS in Japan)
Torque	105lb ft (142Nm) @ 5200rpm
	(110lb ft (149Nm) @ 5200rpm in Japan)
Transmission	5-speed manual (4-sp auto Japan 1985+)
Brakes	Disc/disc
Length/Width/Height	4200/1625/1330mm
Weight	960kg

PERFORMANCE
Max speed (mph)	120
0-60mph (secs)	8.6
Fuel economy (mpg)	32
Desirability	✱ ✱ ✱
Availability	✱ ✱
Tuneability	✱ ✱ ✱

Trying to summarise the spaghetti that is the history of "the world's best-selling car" is frankly pointless and in any case the Corolla's sporting early years were confined to rallying.

The first roadgoing Corolla that enthusiasts acknowledge came in 1983. Launched in Japan as the Corolla Levin or Sprinter Trueno, it was known as the Corolla GT in the UK. Sold in parallel with the deadly-dull 1983-1987 front-wheel drive Corolla, the GT was quite different, offering rear-wheel drive via a live axle located by trailing links and a Panhard rod. It delivered genuinely exciting handling. Indeed, it could be tricky on the limit – but that was all part of the fun. Tellingly, the GT coupé remained Toyota's choice as its rally car during this period. The so-called AE86 series was powered by a lightweight 1.6-litre twin-cam 4A-GEU engine, developing slightly more power in Japanese-spec Sprinter Trueno Apex and Levin GT guise. In Europe, there were two body styles, a two-door coupe and a three-door Liftback. The Japanese Trueno adopted Celica-style pop-up headlamps.

Enthusiasts still adore the AE86 for its delicate handling and tuneability, although rust is a perennial problem.

TOYOTA COROLLA

GTi-16 1987-1992

Second generation AE92 front-wheel drive Corolla GTi was now called GTi-16.

The second generation (AE92) front-wheel drive Corolla GTi was now called GTi-16 to reflect the fact that the 4AGE engine had 16 valves. This was an easy to drive and easy to live with hot hatch, although its ride quality was pretty severe. Performance was quite respectable for its day, too. There was no getting away from the fact that this was a dull-looking car, however.

In 1989, the engine got an extra 6PS and the switchgear and interior trim were changed. European buyers sadly never got the chance to own the supercharged 145PS version that was sold in Japan only.

Subsequent generations of "hot" Corollas lost their way a bit. The 1993-1997 AE102 performance model was tellingly badged GXi and its power dropped down to 120PS, while the 1997-2002 AE111 had even less oomph – 111PS, although it's worth mentioning the G6R limited edition with its six-speed gearbox and side skirts.

SPECIFICATION	
Engine	1587cc 4-cyl
Max power	125PS @ 6600rpm (131PS from 1989)
Torque	107lb ft (145Nm) @ 5000rpm
Transmission	5-speed manual
Brakes	Vented disc/solid disc
Length/Width/Height	3995/1655/1360mm
Weight	990kg
PERFORMANCE	
Max speed (mph)	118
0-60mph (secs)	8.3
Fuel economy (mpg)	34
Desirability	★ ★
Availability	★ ★
Tuneability	★ ★

TOYOTA
COROLLA
T-SPORT 2002-date

The free-revving 192PS engine was easily the best thing about the 2002 Corolla T-Sport.

Having had some sporting cachet, the Corolla descended in the 1990s back to type: a boringly reliable, unexciting hatchback driven by pensioners.

The ninth generation of 2001 was no exception. But then we all got woken up in 2002 with the arrival of the T-Sport. This used the same 192PS engine as the Celica 190, plus a six-speed manual gearbox (and in some markets a four-speed automatic option). This superb VVTi engine let rip above 6000rpm and delivered its 192PS at a screaming 7800rpm.

However the engine was the only exceptional thing about the T-Sport. In every other respect, Toyota did everything possible to dull down any excitement: it looked ordinary, was an average handler and had a very sombre looking cabin. It wasn't even very quick, falling badly behind class leaders like the Honda Civic Type R.

SPECIFICATION	
Engine	1796cc 4-cyl
Max power	192PS @ 7800rpm
Torque	133lb ft (180Nm) @ 6800rpm
Transmission	6-speed manual or 4-speed auto
Brakes	Vented disc/solid disc
Length/Width/Height	4180/1710/1480mm
Weight	1210kg
PERFORMANCE	
Max speed (mph)	140
0-60mph (secs)	8.1
Fuel economy (mpg)	34
Desirability	* *
Availability	* * * *
Tuneability	* * *

TOYOTA CELICA

CELICA & CELICA SUPRA 1981-1986

Toyota invented the Celica badge in 1970 as its medium-sized four-seater coupé. Initially it majored more on style than sportiness, with its "mini-Mustang" styling, and it's outside the scope of this book.

By the third generation, the Celica had established itself as an ultra-popular coupé based on the rear-wheel drive Carina. This version was very 1980s – all sharp-suit styling, black plastic and electronic gizmos. Sold as a notchback (very origami-design) and as a Liftback, pop-up headlamps were a strong design feature.

The UK model's single-carb 2.0-litre engine lacked power, something that was addressed by the Celica Supra. This marked the first use of the Supra name. From the windscreen back, the Celica Supra MA61R shared the Generation 3 Liftback bodywork, but there was an extra six inches up front to fit a 2.8-litre straight six engine with 170PS – making it a direct rival for the Ford Capri 2.8i. Its rear-drive handling was certainly entertaining. The LED digital dashboard fitted to Supras from 1985 frankly looked a mess.

The main problem with this era is the propensity to rust, particularly the roof, tailgate and wings. There are still quite a few around so parts are not an issue, although it's not highly regarded in Celica circles.

Celica Supra used a 170PS 2.8-litre straight six..

SPECIFICATION		
	Celica	Celica Supra
Engine	1972cc 4-cyl	2759cc 6-cyl
Max power	104PS @ 5000rpm	170PS @ 5600rpm
Torque	116lb ft (157Nm) @ 4000rpm	169lb ft (229Nm) @ 4600rpm
Transmission	5-sp manual or 4-sp auto	5-sp manual or 4-sp auto
Brakes	Disc/drum	Disc/disc
Length/Width/Height	4333/1666/1320mm	4620/1684/1320mm
Weight	1170kg	1265kg
PERFORMANCE		
Max speed (mph)	110	128
0-60mph (secs)	10.5	8.1
Fuel economy (mpg)	30	25
Desirability	✱	✱
Availability	✱	✱
Tuneability	✱	✱ ✱

TOYOTA CELICA

1985-1989

In 1985, Toyota switched the Celica to front-drive or, for the GT-Four (pictured), all-wheel drive.

Toyota's landmark Celica has been telling the rest of the world how to do coupés since 1970. By 1985 Toyota had firmly fixed its formula for the future: a front-wheel drive coupé that offered practicality, good looks and reliability.

The Generation 4 ST162 Celica revolutionised Toyota's thinking. Toyota switched to front-wheel drive, gave it a superb new 150PS twin-cam 16-valve 2.0-litre engine and sorted the suspension to give it class-leading handling and poise for the time. The shape was a knockout, with its pop-up headlamps and crisp, sloping fastback.

In Japan, Celicas were marketed in ST, GT and GT-S guises, all available as either coupé or liftback models. STs and GTs came with a 116PS engine, while the GT-S got 140PS. ABS became standard on the 2.0 GT from 1988.

The first Celica convertible was launched in 1987 but only lasted one year, so it remains a rare sight. It had a detachable front roof section, while the rear folded away. It was only sold with manual transmission, no auto.

The most exciting of the Generation 4 Celicas was the GT-Four (ST165), launched in 1986 in Japan and in 1988 in the UK. It featured a turbocharged version of the twin-cam 16V engine that delivered 185PS

TOYOTA CELICA 1985-1989

Toyota has been making the Celica since 1970.

with a catalyst fitted. Its All-Trac permanent four-wheel drive had a 50/50 torque split front to rear that was sensationally grippy for its day. Visually, it featured a deeper front air dam, side skirts and wider wheels and tyres.

Like all Celicas, the ST162 is reliable, simple to maintain and practical. Some spares are becoming harder to find now but plenty of examples are still being broken and there is support from clubs and specialists. Panels are still susceptible to tin worm, while faded and broken plastic trim is common. Definitely avoid the automatic version, which is sluggish and out of character.

SPECIFICATION

	2.0 GT	2.0 GT-Four
Engine	1998cc 4-cyl	1998cc 4-cyl
Max power	150PS @ 6400rpm	185PS @ 6000rpm
Torque	133lb ft (180Nm) @ 4800rpm	184lb ft (250Nm) @ 3600rpm
Transmission	5-speed manual or 4-speed auto	5-speed manual
Brakes	Vented disc/solid disc	Vented disc/solid disc
Length/Width/Height	4365/1710/1290mm	4365/1710/1290mm
Weight	1280kg	1465kg

PERFORMANCE

	2.0 GT	2.0 GT-Four
Max speed (mph)	131	137
0-60mph (secs)	8.5	7.9
Fuel economy (mpg)	34	32
Desirability	* * *	
Availability	* * *	
Tuneability	* * * *	

TOYOTA CELICA
1989-1993

The 1989-1993 Celica was controversially styled but successful. GT-Four is pictured.

At the press conference for the new-shape Celica ST182, a young Jeremy Clarkson asked how Toyota expected to sell such an ugly car. Toyota said there was no problem – and they were right. The Generation 5 ST182, with its curvaceous liftback style and pop-up headlamps, became a best-seller.

Underneath, things remained very much as before. The 2.0 GT engine had slightly more power than before, while in Japan there was the option of hydraulic four-wheel steering and electronic active suspension. Automatic transmission was available until 1992.

There was a convertible again but easily the most exciting model was the ST185 GT-Four. Its turbocharger now boosted power to 204PS and its permanent four-wheel drive featured a viscous centre coupling and Torsen rear differential. Spot it by its wider wings, deep front air dam and bonnet scoops.

Carlos Sainz took the Word Rally Championship in a

Celica GT-Four so Toyota celebrated with a special edition of 5000 (only 440 for the UK). This was called Carlos Sainz in the UK but just RC in Japan (1991-1992). Changes included a new front bumper, extra bonnet ducts, water-cooled intercooler (so power rose by 4PS), weight-saving, better suspension and a short-throw gear lever – as well as a dash plaque and signed certificate.

This generation was too heavy for truly blistering pace and can be expensive on insurance, parts and servicing. But reliability is as solid as ever. The GT-Four gearchange is a little sloppy anyway but there should be no resistance or nasty noises, and no blue smoke from the exhaust when you accelerate. Rust isn't a problem, although paintwork can be. The original 14-inch alloys tend to corrode badly and many owners have replaced them with aftermarket alloys.

SPECIFICATION – EUROPE

	2.0 GT	2.0 GT-Four	2.0 GT-Four Carlos Sainz
Engine	1998cc 4-cyl	1998cc 4-cyl	1998cc 4-cyl
Max power	156PS @ 6600rpm	204PS @ 6000rpm	208PS @ 6000rpm
Torque	137lb ft (186Nm) @ 4800rpm	203lb ft (275Nm) @ 3200rpm	203lb ft (275Nm) @ 3200rpm
Transmission	5-speed manual or 4-speed auto	5-speed manual	5-speed manual
Brakes	Vented disc/solid disc	Vented disc/solid disc	Vented disc/solid disc
Length/Width/Height	4430/1690/1300mm	4430/1690/1300mm	4430/1690/1300mm
Weight	1310kg	1520kg	1520kg
PERFORMANCE			
Max speed (mph)	134	142	143
0-60mph (secs)	8.1	7.9	7.6
Fuel economy (mpg)	35	31	31
Desirability	*	*	*
Availability	*	*	*
Tuneability	*	*	* *

SPECIFICATION – JAPAN

	2.0 GT	2.0 GT-Four	2.0 GT-Four RS
Engine	1998cc 4-cyl	1998cc 4-cyl	1998cc 4-cyl
Max power	165PS @ 6800rpm	225PS @ 6000rpm	235PS @ 6000rpm
Torque	141lb ft (191Nm) @ 4800rpm	224lb ft (304Nm) @ 3200rpm	224lb ft (304Nm) @ 3200rpm
Transmission	5-speed manual or 4-speed auto	5-speed manual	5-speed manual
Brakes	Vented disc/solid disc	Vented disc/solid disc	Vented disc/solid disc
Length/Width/Height	4430/1690/1300mm	4430/1690/1300mm	4430/1690/1300mm
Weight	1310kg	1520kg	1520kg
PERFORMANCE			
Max speed (mph)	134	142	143
0-60mph (secs)	8.0	7.6	7.2
Fuel economy (mpg)	35	31	31
Desirability	*	*	*
Availability	*	*	*
Tuneability	*	*	* *

TOYOTA CELICA

1994-1999

If the Generation 5 Celica was controversially styled, the Generation 6 smoothed the edges: it looked fatter but was in fact lighter and stiffer – and the twin headlamp design was very distinctive, if perhaps a bit gimmicky in retrospect. There was another hike in power for the ST202 2.0-litre engine (up to 175PS) and for the first time the UK also received a 1.8-litre ST entry-level version with 116PS – not in the same league at all – plus a convertible with a standard power soft-top. Minor changes in late 1995 included a new-style rear spoiler.

In Japan, there was a choice of 140PS, 180PS or 200PS 2.0-litre engines and manual or automatic transmission. Most exciting were the 200bhp SS-2 and SS-3 versions (the latter with a bodykit). As before, there was a Celica spin-off called the Curren, which had a notchback rear end and more conventional front-end treatment.

Rally success for Toyota's WRC team – it won the 1993 and 1994 titles – gave birth to the best Celica GT-Four of the lot in February 1994 – the ST205. Lighter weight than the earlier GT-Four helped its cause, as did a much more powerful version of the turbocharged 2.0-litre twin engine (255PS in Japan, 242PS in Europe). Road testers managed to get below six seconds in 0-60 sprints. Its four-wheel drive system imbued it with supercar levels of grip. Bigger brakes with optional ABS and "super strut" suspension also helped it.

The ultimate version is the WRC edition, which was the homologation special (2500 made in total, 1994-1996, all in white). It got an anti-lag valve and water injection (the first road car ever to have these fitted – although they were not actually connected up), plus a larger rear spoiler and bonnet air scoop.

Customer satisfaction surveys show that owners of this generation Celica are a happy bunch – with good reason. There are very few problems and depreciation is low. But you do need a full service history (every 9000 miles) to keep that value up. Front suspension arms are the weakest point – there are three of them (listen for a knocking sound from the front). Grey import GT-Fours have a weaker ceramic turbo shaft, not the steel one on EU cars.

TOYOTA CELICA 1994-1999

The 1994 Celica ST202 – seen here in GT form – was sharp-handling and quick.

The GT-Four was a genuine junior supercar with up to 255PS on tap.

SPECIFICATION – UK

	1.8 ST	2.0 GT	2.0 GT-Four
Engine	1762cc 4-cyl	1998cc 4-cyl	1998cc 4-cyl
Max power	116PS @ 5800rpm	175PS @ 7000rpm	242PS @ 6000rpm
Torque	113lb ft (154Nm) @ 4400rpm	137lb ft (186Nm) @ 4800rpm	224lb ft (304Nm) @ 4000rpm
Transmission	5-speed manual	5-speed manual	5-speed manual
Brakes	Vented disc/solid disc	Vented disc/solid disc	Vented disc/solid disc
Length/Width/Height	4435/1750/1305mm	4435/1750/1305mm	4435/1750/1305mm
Weight	1170kg	1200kg	1400kg
PERFORMANCE			
Max speed (mph)	124	137	153
0-60mph (secs)	10	8.0	6.1
Fuel economy (mpg)	37	34	28
Desirability	*	*	* *
Availability	*	*	*
Tuneability	*	*	* *

SPECIFICATION – JAPAN

	2.0 16v	2.0 SS-II	2.0 GT-Four
Engine	1998cc 4-cyl	1998cc 4-cyl	1998cc 4-cyl
Max power	140PS @ 6000rpm	180PS @ 7000rpm (later 200PS, 170PS w/auto)	255PS @ 6000rpm
Torque	137lb ft (186Nm) @ 4400rpm	140lb ft (191Nm) @ 4800rpm	224lb ft (304Nm) @ 4000rpm
Transmission	5-sp man/4-sp auto	5-sp man/4-sp auto	5-speed manual
Brakes	Vented disc/solid disc	Vented disc/solid disc	Vented disc/solid disc
Length/Width/Height	4435/1750/1305mm	4435/1750/1305mm	4435/1750/1305mm
Weight	1170kg	1190kg	1400kg
PERFORMANCE			
Max speed (mph)	125	137	153
0-60mph (secs)	9.0	7.9	6.1
Fuel economy (mpg)	36	34	28
Desirability	*	*	* *
Availability	*	*	*
Tuneability	*	*	* *

TOYOTA CELICA

1999-date

Californian-designed Celica looked superb. This is a 2004 model.

Another distinct departure for the Celica arrived in 1999 with the radically different-looking Generation 7. In terms of dimensions, it was smaller on the outside but, thanks to its longer wheelbase, bigger for passengers and luggage inside. The shape emerged from Toyota's Californian design studio and won much praise for its lithe contours.

Launched with an all-new 1.8-litre variable valve timing VVTi 143PS engine and six-speed gearbox, the competent chassis cried out for more power. It got just that in 2000 when the 192PS version arrived. This was a cracking engine – a fact proven by its eventual selection by Lotus to power the Elise from 2004. Fairly ordinary at low revs, it hit a Honda VTEC-style "zone" after 6000rpm, exploding in a furious expression of power. A six-speed manual gearbox was standard in the UK.

Toyota later launched a T-Sport 190 version with aero body enhancements and leather trim, which later became the sole high-power model.

It's worth mentioning that, in Japan, two basic models were offered, the SS-I and the SS-II. The former had the 143PS engine but a five-speed manual or four-speed automatic transmission. The SS-II was the sportier model, with a six-speed manual gearbox (and later the 192PS engine), which was also available with a "Super Strut Package" which added even more sportiness and shaved 20kg off the overall weight.

Toyota's bullet-proof reliability record shows no sign of waning in the latest-generation Celica, with satisfaction surveys again putting the Toyota coupé close to the top slot. No major problems are reported, even with an engine developing more than 100PS per litre, although it needs regular oil changes. There are a few Japanese imports out there, so check you're buying a genuine car with a full service history.

SPECIFICATION

	1.8 VVTi 140	1.8 VVTi 190
Engine	1796cc 4-cyl	1796cc 4-cyl
Max power	143PS @ 6400rpm	192PS @ 7800rpm
Torque	125lb ft (170Nm) @ 4200rpm	133lb ft (180Nm) @ 6800rpm
Transmission	6-sp man (5-sp man /4-sp auto Japan)	6-sp man (4-sp auto option Japan)
Brakes	Vented disc/solid disc	Vented disc/solid disc
Length/Width/Height	4335/1735/1305mm	4335/1735/1305mm
Weight	1155kg	1215kg

PERFORMANCE

Max speed (mph)	127	140
0-60mph (secs)	8.4	7.2
Fuel economy (mpg)	36	33
Desirability	★ ★ ★	
Availability	★ ★ ★	★ ★
Tuneability	★ ★ ★	

TOYOTA SUPRA

1986-1993

Toyota had introduced the Supra name on the Celica Supra of 1981, but its 1986 replacement dropped the Celica tag, reflecting the fact that this was an all-new stand-alone car in a class above the Celica.

The MA70 series Supra was a far more portly car, weighing over 1.5 tonnes. That sumo wrestler weight was partly down to being laden with so many gadgets: UK cars all had air conditioning, electric windows, memory steering adjustment and cruise control, for example.

The new Supra looked quite handsome in an Americanesque sort of way, with its pop-up headlamps and sloping glass tail. In feel it was more of a cruiser than a true sports car, despite its all-round independent suspension and firm ride. The rear-wheel drive chassis was simply not in the same class as rivals such as the 1989 Nissan 300ZX.

In Europe, the engine was a 3.0-litre straight six with a single overhead cam and 24 valves. As launched in 1986, it had 204PS, but this dropped in 1989 to 187PS when a catalyst was added. In compensation, Toyota launched a Supra Turbo the same year boasting a single turbocharger and an output of 235PS – good enough for supercar-belittling performance. A 1988 facelift mildly altered the front end styling.

Japanese market Supras were rather more diverse. You could buy a 2.0-litre six-cylinder engine with or without twin turbocharging (between 135PS and 210PS), or the 3.0-litre engine with a turbocharger, offering 240PS in standard tune or 270PS in Evolution Turbo-A Limited spec. In 1990 power was boosted even higher when a new 2.5-litre twin turbocharged 1JZ-GTE engine arrived (with 280PS). The Twin Turbo-R final model got Bilstein dampers and a Torsen limited slip differential. Japanese buyers could also choose a targa model with removable roof panels.

It may have been overweight, but the Supra could be a quick performer, especially in Turbo guise (pictured).

SPECIFICATION	Supra	Supra Turbo	Supra 2.5 GT Turbo (Japan)
Engine	2954cc 6-cyl	2954cc 6-cyl	2491cc 6-cyl
Max power	204PS @ 6000rpm (187PS 1989+)	235PS @ 5600rpm	280PS @ 6200rpm
Torque	187lb ft (254Nm) @ 4800rpm	253lb ft (344Nm) @ 3200rpm	267lb ft (363Nm) @ 4800rpm
Transmission	5-speed manual or 3-speed automatic with overdrive		
Brakes	Vented disc/vented disc	Vented disc/vented disc	Vented disc/vented disc
Length/Width/Height	4620/1690/1300mm	4620/1690/1300mm	4620/1690/1300mm
Weight	1545kg	1570kg	1520kg
PERFORMANCE			
Max speed (mph)	136	152	155
0-60mph (secs)	8.0	6.1	5.7
Fuel economy (mpg)	29	26	23
Desirability	★	★	
Availability	★	★	★
Tuneability	★	★	★ ★

TOYOTA SUPRA

1993-1999

European Supras were always Twin Turbo, though this is a rare example without a rear spoiler.

Toyota has never made a faster car than the JZA80 Supra. When it arrived in 1993 to replace the long-running MA70, it was greeted as something of a wide-boy's car because of its brash character, twin-turbo engine and relatively unrefined chassis. But there was no denying it was packed with equipment, offered devastating performance – 158mph and 0-60 in 5.1 seconds – and had lots of grip.

According to official Japanese figures, the 2JZ-GTE six-cylinder 3.0-litre twin-sequential-turbo engine pumped out 280PS. The suspicion that Japanese outputs were actually a lot higher was borne out when virtually the same engine was listed in European markets as having 330PS.

The first turbocharger kicked in at 2000rpm to minimise lag while the second turbo did not start spooling until 4500rpm. The 2JZ-GTE engine later featured BEAMS and VVT-i which electronically controlled the timing of the intake camshaft to optimise throttle response, low-end power and emissions. There were also twin ceramic turbine-wheels in the turbo.

In the UK, the 2+2 Supra was fitted with plenty of luxuries like air conditioning, cruise control, power driver's seat and traction control. A six-speed Getrag manual gearbox was probably the best choice but there was also a four-speed automatic option. This was a sizzlingly quick car, all the more amazing because it was so heavy, at over 1.5 tons. And Toyota had even tried to make it lightweight with items like hollow carpet fibres and a hollow (optional) rear spoiler.

While the Supra disappeared from the UK in May 1996, in Japan it carried on going until 1999. The Japanese model came in a number of different versions but undoubtedly the best were the twin turbocharged ones, badged RZ or GZ. The RZ had the six-speed manual and Bilstein dampers while the RZ-S was also offered with a four-speed automatic with ETC-iS

SPECIFICATION		
	RZ/GZ (twin turbo)	SZ (non-turbo)
Engine	2997cc 6-cyl	2997cc 6-cyl
Max power	280PS @ 5600rpm (330PS in EU)	225PS @ 6000rpm
Torque	315lb ft (441Nm) @ 3600rpm	210lb ft (284Nm) @ 4800rpm
Transmission	6-speed manual (5-speed in some markets) or 4-speed automatic	
Brakes	Vented disc/vented disc	Vented disc/vented disc
Length/Width/Height	4520/1810/1275mm	4520/1810/1275mm
Weight	1510kg	1410kg
PERFORMANCE		
Max speed (mph)	158	143
0-60mph (secs)	5.1	6.5
Fuel economy (mpg)	18	20
Desirability	★★★★	★
Availability	★★★★	★
Tuneability	★★★★	★

(steering wheel buttons for manual shifts). The GZ also had the twin turbo engine but a more luxurious specification and either five-speed manual or four-speed auto transmission.

There was also a normally-aspirated 2JZ-GE version of the 3.0-litre engine with SZ badging. It developed a lot less power at 225PS, came with either five-speed manual or four-speed automatic transmission and had less complete equipment levels. There was also an Aerotop version of the SZ with lift-out glass roof panels for semi-open air motoring. The SZ-R version had the six-speed manual gearbox and limited slip differential.

From 1997, the RZ and SZ-R were equipped with newly-developed REAS damping (Relative Absorber System) that was effectively a fully-adjustable suspension system using hydraulic fluid and gas. 1997 also saw minor revisions to the head and tail-lights, chassis modifications and extra sound-deadening. From 1998 VVT-i appeared on the non-turbo engine but the following year Supra production ceased.

Many Japanese-market Supras were ordered with a dramatic Type R body kit, featuring a wild rear spoiler and an active front spoiler that achieved a Cd figure of 0.30. After-market bodykits were hugely popular too, some of them (like Veilside's) looking utterly phantasmagorical, with tortured side skirts and extreme rear spoilers. Whether you appreciate the "taste" of these is a matter of personal choice.

Many owners have neglected their steeds and many have been heavily modified, so you need to take care when buying. Prices start amazingly low for such a high-performance car. Parts prices are pretty reasonable too, although insurance and fuel costs can be high.

Toyota's mechanicals are pretty well bullet-proof but the service history with turbo cars needs to have all its Ts crossed. In particular, neglected oil changes can mean trouble for the turbocharger. Check for worn leather upholstery, malfunctioning electrics, expensive-to-fix gearbox problems (difficult-to-engage gears and nasty noises), heavy tyre wear, juddering brakes and a noisy differential. Engines have been known to overheat, too.

Giant-slaying pace from the 330PS Supra engine. This is a late-model Japanese-spec Supra.

TOYOTA SOARER
(LEXUS SC) 1991-2000

Soarer is a name that has been applied to Toyota's grandest coupé since 1981. The world didn't sit up and pay attention until 1991, however, when an all-new generation transformed Japanese luxury coupé fortunes in a single stroke.

In Japan this car was called the Toyota Soarer, but in the USA it was sold wearing the Lexus SC badge. It was never officially imported to Europe, although it served to trailblaze the Japanese grey import market in Britain.

The Soarer's lines were understated, its cabin was luxurious and its engineering as complete as any Japanese car. With a superb ride, faultless build quality, finely-tuned rear-wheel drive handling and more electronic gizmos than you shake a modem at, it was a high-quality car across a wide range of measures.

Three engines were offered. The entry level was a 225PS 3.0-litre straight six. The sportiest was a 2.5-litre twin turbo, which boasted 280PS and a free-revving nature. The top of the range cruiser was the 260PS 4.0-litre V8 – basically the same engine as used in the Lexus LS400 saloon.

Technically very sophisticated, most Soarers had switchable traction control, adjustable ride height and four-wheel steering. The top 4.0GT models even came

SPECIFICATION			
	4.0	**3.0**	**2.5GT**
Engine	3969cc V8	2997cc 6-cyl	2491cc 6-cyl
Max power	260PS @ 5400rpm	225-230PS @ 6000rpm	280PS @ 6200rpm
Torque	267lb ft (363Nm) @ 4600rpm	224lb ft (304Nm) @ 4800rpm	278lb ft (378Nm) @ 2400rpm
Transmission	5-speed manual or 4-speed auto	5-speed manual or 4-speed auto	5-speed manual or 4-speed auto
Brakes	Vented disc/vented disc	Vented disc/vented disc	Vented disc/vented disc
Length/Width/Height	4860/1790/1340mm	4860/1790/1340mm	4860/1790/1340mm
Weight	1630kg	1630kg	1630kg
PERFORMANCE			
Max speed (mph)	143	136	147
0-60mph (secs)	6.9	7.9	6.6
Fuel economy (mpg)	18	21	20
Desirability	★	★	
Availability	★	★	★
Tuneability	★	★	

with hydraulic active suspension, while many had an LCD centre console to house the air conditioning controls, satellite navigation and TV. There was a minor facelift in 1996 but otherwise the Soarer continued unabated until 2000.

To drive, all Soarers feel more relaxed than sporty, despite Toyota reportedly changing the engine's sound to make it more noisy! Used examples can be picked up at bargain prices because they have a slightly wide-boy image these days, and are not as exciting to drive as many Japanese coupés. Look for a full service record, malfunctioning TV display and complex electronics, while you should avoid nasty bodykits and white paintwork.

The Toyota Soarer (Lexus SC400 in the USA) was more of a grand tourer than a performance icon.

TOYOTA SOARER
(LEXUS SC430) 2001-date

Hardtop roof folds electrically into the boot.

Toyota struck out in another new direction with its replacement for the long-running Lexus SC. The all-new SC430 (still badged Toyota Soarer in Japan) brought a convertible roof to the luxury coupé format for the first time. The hardtop roof folded electrically into the boot, opening the 2+2 cabin to the elements.

Was this a performance car? Perhaps not, but it was certainly fast – in a middle-aged executive kind of way. 0-60mph in 6.2 seconds remains impressively rapid, although cornering was distinctly soft.

Whatever its image, the SC430 was subject to unprecedented demand at launch, and at last European buyers could own a Lexus coupé. A plush UK spec included leather, wood, power seats, lap-jet warm air flow and a Mark Levinson audio system.

SPECIFICATION	
Engine	4293cc V8
Max power	286PS @ 5600rpm (304PS in US)
Torque	309lb ft (419Nm) @ 3500rpm (324lb ft (440Nm) in US)
Transmission	5-speed automatic
Brakes	Vented disc/vented disc
Length/Width/Height	4515/1830/1370mm
Weight	1720kg
PERFORMANCE	
Max speed (mph)	155
0-60mph (secs)	6.2
Fuel economy (mpg)	23
Desirability	* * * *
Availability	* *
Tuneability	* *

TOYOTA SOARER / LEXUS SC430 2001-DATE

Known as the Soarer in Japan but Lexus SC430 elsewhere, this was Toyota's first-ever big convertible.

The American Champ Car racing series used the Lexus SC430 as a pace car. The one-off car featured at tuned engine with 312bhp and modified suspension.

TOYOTA ALTEZZA
(LEXUS IS) 1998-2005

Lexus IS200 was sold with a turbo engine in Japan as the Altezza RS200.

Lexus had successfully inculcated itself as a luxury brand in Europe and the USA with the LS400 but its image was rather middle-aged and staid. The IS200, launched in 1998, changed all that.

Here was a rear-wheel drive BMW 3 Series competitor that looked the part and felt sporty too. Its sharp design was punctuated by charismatic rear lights, while its high quality interior featured Swiss watch style dials. It had a fluid and inspiring chassis with delightfully light steering and brakes as sharp as any rival's.

In Europe the IS200 was launched in one form only, with a 2.0-litre straight six engine. The 3.0-litre IS300 joined it in 2001 powered by the six-cylinder 2JZ-GE VVTi engine. There was standard five-speed automatic transmission in Europe but a five-speed manual was sold in other markets. A supercharged IS200 with 186PS was also available in some countries (but not the UK), while a SportCross estate was launched in 2002 (called Altezza Gita in Japan).

In Japan, the IS200 was launched as the Toyota Altezza (where it was 1998/99 Japanese Car of the Year). The Altezza was offered not only with the six-cylinder engine (badged AS200 and in automatic only) but also (badged RS200) with a four-cylinder BEAMS VVTi 2.0-litre twin cam engine. In six-speed manual RS200 form, there was an amazing 210PS – a specific output of 105PS per litre. This unit revved deep into the 7000rpm range – not quite Honda VTEC territory but the variable valvegear sounded more and more like a race car as you edged up to the red line. The RS200 came with a six-speed manual or five-speed semi-auto transmission. The latter had F1-style steering wheel buttons to move up and down ratios.

TOYOTA ALTEZZA / LEXUS IS 1998-2005

The 3.0-litre IS300 arrived in 2001 with the six-cylinder 2JZ-GE VVTi engine.

A stylish and high-quality interior helped the IS200 compete with European rivals such as the BMW 3-series.

SPECIFICATION				
	Lexus IS200	**Lexus IS300**	**Altezza AS200**	**Altezza RS200**
Engine	1988cc 6-cyl	2997cc 6-cyl	1988cc 6-cyl	1998cc 4-cyl
Max power	155PS @ 6200rpm	214PS @ 5800rpm	160PS @ 6200rpm	210PS @ 7600rpm (200PS @ 7000rpm auto)
Torque	143lb ft (195Nm) @ 4600rpm	212lb ft (288Nm) @ 3800rpm	147lb ft (200Nm) @ 4400rpm	159lb ft (215Nm) @ 6400rpm
Transmission	6-sp manual or 4-sp auto	5-sp auto (or 5-sp manual outside EU)	4-speed auto	6-speed manual or 5-speed auto
Brakes	Vented disc/solid disc	Vented disc/solid disc	Vented disc/solid disc	Vented disc/solid disc
Length/Width/Height	4400/1720/1410mm	4400/1720/1410mm	4400/1720/1410mm	4400/1720/1410mm
Weight	1400kg	1510kg	1310kg	1270kg
PERFORMANCE				
Max speed (mph)	134	143	140	140
0-60mph (secs)	9.5	8.2	8.0	7.2
Fuel economy (mpg)	29	26	29	28
Desirability	*	*	*	
Availability	*	*	*	* *
Tuneability	*	*	*	*

TOYOTA
ARISTO
V300 1991-1997

Hugely powerful V300 version of the Toyota Aristo (Lexus GS300) made it a Merc AMG rival.

Aristo is the curious Japanese market name for a car sold worldwide as the Lexus GS300. The first generation, launched in Japan in late 1991, was designed by Giugiaro and certainly looked handsome. But in a market dominated by the BMW 5 Series, its dynamics were lacking. As well as the normal 3.0-litre six-cylinder engine, Japan got a high-performance twin-turbo model with 280PS (and a 4.0-litre 260PS V8 with four-wheel steer).

It was not until the second generation GS300 of 1997 that Toyota's saloon really grew up. Its normally-aspirated 3.0-litre straight-six engine offered 220PS in European tune. But Japanese buyers could opt for a 280PS twin-turbocharged version. Called the Aristo V300, it also boasted nearly 50 per cent more torque at lower revs.

This has obvious implications for the driving experience. Not only does it make a more comfortable car to pilot at low revs, the V300 explodes when you floor the accelerator from the mid-range when the turbos cut in. At the top end it will comfortably exceed 150mph.

There were also two high-specification models. First was the Vertex Edition, with its upgraded interior, special wheels and rear spoiler, plus optional paddle-shift controls on the steering wheel. If you wanted a sportier feel the TTE-equipped model (Toyota Team Europe) got a variety of goodies such as fat 18-inch alloy wheels, Bilstein suspension and a sports exhaust system. It's an undiscovered performance bargain.

SPECIFICATION

Engine	2997cc 6-cyl
Max power	280PS @ 5600rpm
Torque	318lb ft (430Nm) @ 3600rpm
Transmission	5-speed automatic
Brakes	Vented disc/vented disc
Length/Width/Height	4865/1795/1430mm
Weight	1680kg

PERFORMANCE

Max speed (mph)	150
0-60mph (secs)	6.6
Fuel economy (mpg)	21
Desirability	* * *
Availability	* *
Tuneability	* * *

TOYOTA MR2
Mk1 1984-1989

Pundits called the MR2 Mk1 a mini-Ferrari – remarkably, that wasn't an exaggeration.

MR2's bodyshell was incredibly stiff thanks to no less than five bulkheads.

Arguably the best mass-produced mid-engined car of all time is Toyota's MR2. When it was launched in 1984, the MR2 (Midship Runabout 2-seater) was an extremely bold move. The only other popular mid-engined car at the time was the archaic Fiat X1/9, while Japan had never built a mid-engined road car before.

Unlike most other sports cars, the MR2 had a very broad appeal based on a practical, comfortable layout, strong performance, superb handling and fine build quality. In engineering terms, the engine and many other components were borrowed (the 1600 engine and transaxle came from the Corolla GT).

The so-called AW11 MR2 Mk1's bodyshell was extremely stiff thanks to no less than five bulkheads. Four-cylinder engines were compact in size and mated to a five-speed manual transmission (plus an optional four-speed automatic in some markets). Twin gearchange cables provided the sort of smooth gearshift that other mid-engined cars would have killed for. MacPherson struts, offset coil springs and gas-filled dampers, anti-roll bars, quick steering and all-round disc brakes completed an impressive brief.

Initially it was available only on the home market in three guises: a base 1500S, the 1600G and the 1600G-Limited; the 130PS 1600 models were the "real" MR2s. The MR2 was named Japan's Car of the Year for 1984/85. Europeans waited until March 1985 to sample the delights of the MR2 in 124PS 1600 form but sadly not the 145PS supercharged MR2 launched in Japan in 1986. All markets got the T-Bar roof MR2 with its removable glass roof panels and the suspension/braking package of the supercharged MR2.

Some enthusiasts regard the Mk1 MR2 as a superior handler to the bulkier Mk2. It's certainly still a common sight, and despite some rust problems, it's a very reliable car. Electrical gremlins can strike though, notably the mirrors, windows and hi-fi.

SPECIFICATION

	1.6 Europe	1.5 Japan	1.6 Japan	1.6 supercharged
Engine	1587cc 4-cyl	1452cc 4-cyl	1587cc 4-cyl	1587cc 4-cyl
Max power	124PS @ 6600rpm (116PS with catalyst)	83PS @ 5600rpm	130PS @ 6600rpm (120PS from 1986)	145PS @ 6400rpm
Torque	105lb ft (142Nm) @ 5000rpm	87lb ft (117Nm) @ 3600rpm	110lb ft (149Nm) @ 5200rpm (105lb ft (142Nm) from 1986)	137lb ft (186Nm) @ 4400rpm
Transmission	5-speed manual	5-speed manual or 4-speed auto	5-speed manual or 4-speed auto	5-speed manual or 4-speed auto
Brakes	Vented disc/solid disc	Solid disc/solid disc	Vented disc/solid disc	Vented disc/solid disc
Length/Width/Height	3925/1665/1250mm	3925/1665/1250mm	3925/1665/1250mm	3925/1665/1250mm
Weight	1010kg	960kg	1000kg	1070kg
PERFORMANCE				
Max speed (mph)	124	106	124	130
0-60mph (secs)	7.7	11	7.7	7.2
Fuel economy (mpg)	36	38	36	32
Desirability	★	★	★	
Availability	★	★	★	★
Tuneability	★	★	★	★

TOYOTA MR2
Mk2 1989-1999

Power of the MR2 GT went from 161PS to 174PS in 1994.

MR2 was phenomenally successful. Pictured is a 10th Anniversary edition.

The MR2 Mk1 had been so successful that Toyota was in confident mood to produce a successor. In October 1989 it launched the all-new second-generation MR2 (SW20 series). Larger, heavier, more powerful and more up-market, the MR2 suited the times. The styling was also more contemporary, with a longer, sleeker, more rounded shape.

A new range of 2.0-litre engines borrowed from the Celica ST182 gave even the base MR2 165PS in Japan. The suspension was completely revised, larger wheels and tyres were specified and the brakes were more powerful (ABS was a popular option). Toyota employed the services of American race driver Dan Gurney to tune the handling but wet-weather break-aways could give drivers a nasty shock.

This handling trait was most marked on a powerful new Turbo version. Badged GT, it featured a twin-entry ceramic turbocharger and intercooler (shared with the Celica GT-Four) pumping out 225PS in its initial guise, rising to 235PS after 1992 and 245PS after 1994. That enabled Toyota to claim junior supercar status with a 149mph top speed and 0-60mph in 5.9 seconds.

The Turbo model was only ever a "grey" import in Europe (the USA received a 2.2-litre 130PS MR2 as well as a 200PS version of the Turbo engine). The European market base model used the Carina's dowdy 2.0-litre 121PS engine, but far more popular was the GT with its 161PS engine. As before, closed-roof and T-Bar versions were available and for the first time in Europe, the option of automatic transmission.

The aforementioned handling problems were finally resolved in a raft of changes introduced in

TOYOTA MR2 MK2 1989-1999

Second generation MR2 grew up substantially. This is a GT T-Bar.

1992. The suspension gained stiffer anti-roll bars front and rear, the dampers were retuned to a stiffer setting, ride height was reduced by 10mm and the lower rear suspension arms were lengthened. Coupled with larger 15-inch wheels, fatter tyres and better steering, the MR2 was far safer. The 121PS MR2 was dropped the same year. Another major set of changes occurred in 1994: the power output rose to 174PS, and all models gained ABS and a minor styling update. A final minor facelift occurred in 1998.

A very rare official MR2 delicacy was the MR Spider, produced by an offshoot of Toyota Racing Development (TRD) from 1996. This was an exceptionally neat full soft-top 200PS MR2 with a Ferrari Spider-type hood and twin head fairings over the engine cover.

MR2s do need proper servicing and a full service history is vital. Accident damage is common. Reliability is excellent but wear inevitably takes its toll on the clutch, brakes and gearchange quality.

SPECIFICATION

	Europe 2.0	2.0 GT Europe	G (Japan)	GT/GTS (Japan)
Engine	1998cc 4-cyl	1998cc 4-cyl	1998cc 4-cyl	1998cc 4-cyl
Max power	121PS @ 5600rpm	161PS @ 6800rpm	165PS @ 6800rpm (180PS 1993+, 200PS 1997+)	225PS @ 6000rpm (235PS 1992+, 245PS 1994+)
Torque	130lb ft (176Nm) @ 4400rpm	141lb ft (191Nm) @ 4800rpm	141lb ft (191Nm) @ 4800rpm	224lb ft (304Nm) @ 4000rpm
Transmission	5-sp manual or 4-sp auto	5-sp manual	5-sp manual or 4-sp auto	5-sp manual
Brakes	Vented disc/vented disc	Vented disc/vented disc	Vented disc/vented disc	Vented disc/vented disc
Length/Width/Height	4180/1695/1240mm	4180/1695/1240mm	4180/1695/1240mm	4180/1695/1240mm
Weight	1145kg	1210kg	1210kg	1260kg
PERFORMANCE				
Max speed (mph)	124	140	140	149
0-60mph (secs)	9.1	7.2	7.0	5.9
Fuel economy (mpg)	37	35	35	29
Desirability	*	*	*	*
Availability	*	*	*	*
Tuneability	*	*	*	*

TOYOTA MR2
ROADSTER 1999-date

In October 1999 the all-new third-generation MR2 (MR-S in Japan) made its international debut. Its bold new styling announced a revolution: the MR2 Roadster was a full convertible. The soft-top folded neatly by hand and even had a heated glass rear window (an optional hardtop being a popular item).

Sharp angles, extended wheelarches, prominent side air dams and cowled headlamps refreshed the MR2's appeal. It was a whole 12 inches shorter than the old MR2 and much lighter – even lighter in fact than the first-generation MR2.

The 140PS 1.8-litre VVTL-i engine was shared with the Celica and Toyota claimed the best power-to-weight ratio of any car in its class (discounting the Lotus Elise). The rear suspension was an all-new design of dual links and struts and resulted in sublime handling. With so little weight over the front wheels, the steering was ultra-direct and turn-in was almost as crisp as an Elise. The transition to and from oversteer was mild and predictable - fun, not frantic – although the ride quality was pretty firm.

The only transmission choice initially was a five-speed manual. An SMT (sequential manual transmission) was offered from 2000 with steering wheel buttons to change gear, but it was not widely liked.

Inside, a pared-down minimalist cabin featured tubular metal door handles echoed in vertical centre console rails. Practicality took a back seat – literally – as the only luggage space was directly behind the seats.

A mid-life update in 2002 brought a six-speed gearbox (both manual and SMT), standard Vehicle Stability Control Traction Control on the SMT, improved suspension, 16-inch rear wheels and restyled headlamps and rear lamps.

Back to basics: ultra-light third generation MR2 lost its top.

TOYOTA MR2 ROADSTER 1999-DATE

SPELIFICATION

Engine	1795cc 4-cyl
Max power	140PS @ 6400rpm
Torque	127lb ft (171Nm) @ 4400rpm
Transmission	5-sp man (6-sp from 2002) or 5-sp/6-sp sequential manual
Brakes	Vented disc/vented disc
Length/Width/Height	3885/1695/1235mm
Weight	1010kg (SMT 1045kg)

PERFORMANCE

Max speed (mph)	130
0-60mph (secs)	7.7 (SMT 9.1 secs)
Fuel economy (mpg)	37
Desirability	✴ ✴ ✴ ✴
Availability	✴ ✴ ✴ ✴
Tuneability	✴ ✴ ✴

This Zagato-styled MR2 VM180 was based on the Japanese-market MR2 with 155PS.

Optional hardtop restored some practicality.

TOYOTA

Other Models

The Paseo (Cynos in Japan).

Seductive 2000GT was Toyota's first genuine sports car.

Toyota boasted a sports car in its range as early as 1965 with the launch of the **Sports 800** but the numeral gives the game away: with an air-cooled two-cylinder 800cc engine it was hardly powerful. And its spec was ultra-conservative: torsion bar front end, rigid rear axle with semi-elliptics, drum brakes and worm and sector steering.

The **2000GT** of 1967 was the first full-blooded Toyota sports car, a quite stunning machine masterfully styled by Count Albrecht Goertz. Yamaha designed and built the glorious twin cam 1988cc six-cylinder engine (indeed they built the whole car), in its highest state of tune delivering 200bhp. Japanese go mad for the 2000GT and pay a fortune because only 337 were ever made.

As the Corolla passed through its various incarnations, Toyota consistently produced sportier sister models under the names **Corolla Levin** and **Corolla Sprinter** with slightly different bodywork. The 1983 series **Sprinter Trueno**, for example, was a Corolla GT with pop-up headlamps. The 1999 **Corolla Levin BZ-R** is also worthy of note, a smart coupé with 165PS and a six-speed transmission.

One of Toyota's best-known niche models is the **Sera**, a four-seater coupé with one unique party piece. To get in, you lifted a gullwing door, each of which featured wraparound glass to create a bubble-top effect. It may have been based on the humble Starlet, but its 1.5-litre 110PS engine allowed a top speed of 121mph. Used prices start very low and there's even an owner's club (www.toyotasera.com). About 15,000 were made between 1990 and 1994.

The **Cynos** coupé was launched in Japan in 1991 but didn't make it to the UK until 1996, badged as the **Paseo**. This was a frankly lame front-wheel drive coupé with old technology (beam rear suspension for goodness' sake) and a mere 1.5-litre engine (105-115PS in Japan and just 91PS in the UK). If you're into performance cars, avoid this one!

The **Yaris T-Sport** has been marketed as a hot hatch but in truth its 105PS 1.5-litre engine was never more than lukewarm. In Japan the hottest version was badged as the Vitz RS.

Thought the GT-Four name died with the Celica ST205? Bizarrely, it was revived in 2004 on an estate car! The **Caldina GT-Four** had a turbocharged 3S-GTE 2.0-litre engine with 260PS and four-wheel drive. But, proving this was no sports car, it only came with four-speed automatic transmission.

Gullwing, bubble-top Sera was a curiosity rather than a performance car.

SPECIALISTS

The Gigliato Aerosa was once earmarked to be made by Lamborghini.

AUTOBACS GARAIYA
Autobacs is Japan's largest car parts retailer and in 2002, it unveiled the Garaiya sports car. This Porsche Boxster rival housed a Nissan SR20VE 2.0-litre mid-mounted engine and six-speed gearbox in a dramatically swoopy coupé body. Production was not scheduled to begin until mid-2005, at a factory in the UK.

Autobacs Garaiya used a mid-mounted Nissan engine.

GIGLIATO AEROSA
Founded in 1987 by ex-Isuzu designer Nobuo Nakamura, Gigliato Design created the handsome Aerosa sports coupé was in 1989. A production-ready car was launched at the 1993 Frankfurt Motor Show. It used a Ford V6 3.0-litre 220PS engine, mounted centrally and mated to a five-speed gearbox. Its tubular chassis was clothed in aluminium stressed panels and glassfibre bodywork. Gigliato first announced its intention to build cars in the UK, then in 1997 paired up with Lamborghini, by which time it had a 4.6-litre 330PS V8 engine mounted longitudinally. Audi's acquisition of Lamborghini scuppered the project.

JIOTTO CASPITA
Curiously the major funder for the Jiotto Caspita supercar project was an underwear manufacturer called Wacoal. The Group C-style Caspita made its

SPECIALISTS

Mitsuoka Zero 1 was a Lotus Seven lookalike based on the Mazda MX-5

debut at the 1989 Tokyo Motor Show. Initial plans called for a modified 3.5-litre flat-12 450PS Formula 1 racing engine from Motori Moderni/Subaru. However by 1991 the company intended to use a Nissan Infiniti 32-valve V8 engine and in 1992 that had changed again to a Judd 3.5-litre V10 engine. Despite announcing a launch price of $650,000, production never began.

MITSUOKA

Obtaining an official licence to produce cars in Japan is a very difficult task, but Mitsuoka succeeded in becoming Japan's 10th car constructor in 1993. It started out making microcars and pastiches of classic British cars, usually based on Nissans. The 1994 Zero 1 was its most serious product, a Caterham 7 inspired sports car based on Mazda MX-5 mechanicals, including its 120PS 1.6-litre engine. All-independent suspension fitted into a tubular chassis clothed in aluminium panels, much like the Caterham. This successful model was followed up in 1996 by the Classic Type F, an updated version of the Zero 1 with an Alfa Tipo-style front end. The 740kg heavy car was fitted with a 130PS Mazda 1.8-litre engine. Mitsuoka has since shown a prototype called Orochi, a supercar coupé that has not yet entered production.

SARD MC-8

The famous Sard racing company made the MC-8 in the 1990s, a rebodying exercise on the second-generation Toyota MR2. The wheelbase was lengthened by 460mm (18 inches) to accommodate a 260PS 4.0-litre Lexus V8 engine mounted centrally. The front and rear bodywork was completely changed.

TOMMY KAIRA

Japanese engineer Kikuo Kaira gave his name, in conjunction with the tuning house, Tomita, in creating the Tommy Kaira ZZ in 1995. This was a mid-engined two-seater in the Lotus Elise vein, powered by a Nissan 2.0-litre 185PS engine. Because of its light weight, Tomita claimed a 0-60mph time of just 4.6 seconds. The ZZ was actually built in Norfolk, England although most of the 200 or so produced were exported to Japan. However, the Japanese recession forced it out of production in 1999. Tomita was taken over by Autobacs in 2001, which continued to offer the ZZ to special order and also produced a ZZ-II prototype in advance of its own Garaiya sports car. By that time, licence production of the ZZ had begun at the UK company Leading Edge Sports Car Company, which offered it as the Leading Edge RT190 and RT240.

VEMAC

The Vemac RD180 was another Japanese/British co-production. Built from 1998, it looked like a coupé but its hardtop detached to make a roadster. It used a 180PS 1.8-litre VTEC engine from the Honda Integra mounted centrally plus a five-speed gearbox with the lever mounted on the right-hand sill. It weighed only 940kg so performance was peppy. Great handling was also assured by being engineered by the same team that made Gordon Murray's Rocket in the 1990s. Further models included the RD200 (Honda 2.0 engine), RD320 and RD350.

YAMAHA OX99-II

Although Yamaha is a world famous name for its motorbikes, the Japanese giant had a stab at supercar manufacture with the dramatic OX99-II. The centrepiece was its engine, a 3.5-litre V12 engine taken directly from Formula 1. The 400PS engine mounted directly to the carbon-fibre/aluminium monocoque chassis and drove through a six-speed transmission. The dramatic coupé body was hand-formed in aluminium, and featured a tandem two-seater layout. Much publicity was afforded the prototype in 1992, with Yamaha saying that production was due to begin in 1993 or 1994 at a British subsidiary of Yamaha's, Ypsilon Technology Ltd of Milton Keynes. But the OX99-II was a victim of the downturn in supercar fortunes in the early 1990s and no customer cars were ever made.